In Search of Islands
A Life of Conor O'Brien

Judith Hill

The Collins Press

PUBLISHED IN 2009 BY
The Collins Press
West Link Park
Doughcloyne
Wilton
Cork

British Library Cataloguing in Publication Data

Hill, Judith
    Conor O'Brien : in search of the islands
    1. O'Brien, Conor, 1880-1952 2. Sailors - Ireland - Biography
    3. Voyages around the world 4. Ireland - Biography
    I. Title
    941.7'082'092
    ISBN-13: 9781905172658

Book design and layout by Copper Reed Studio
Typeset in Palatino and Futura
Printed in China by PrintWORKS

Contents

'Man is born homeless, and shaped for the sea.'
From *Ithaca*, Theo Dorgan

Acknowledgements

This book began with Gary MacMahon's enthusiasm for Conor O'Brien and for Irish traditional boats. He had done ten years' work researching O'Brien's boats and collecting photographs, drawings, letters and first editions of O'Brien's books when he asked me if I would be interested in writing a biography. He had also known Murrogh O'Brien, Conor's nephew, and Murrogh's wife, Suzanne, for several years and they had given the project of writing about O'Brien's life their wholehearted support. I began the research with their encouragement and enjoyed several sessions talking to them about their memories of Conor, and looking at family photographs and paintings. Gary was a constant source of inspiration about Conor, while his knowledge of sailing and the sea has kept the book afloat. I am grateful to the O'Brien family for lending me material and for permitting me to quote from Conor's writings. I am also grateful to Theo Dorgan for giving me permission to quote from his poem, 'Ithaca'.

I have had information and assistance from many quarters: Pádraig de Bhaldraithe, John Cussen, Colette Ellison (Royal Society of Antiquaries of Ireland), Michael Finucane, Suzanne Foster (archivist, Winchester College), Colin Harris (Bodleian Library, Oxford), Captain Roger Heptinstall RN, Brian Hodkinson (Jim Kemmy Municipal Museum, Limerick), Clare Hopkins (archivist, Trinity College, Oxford), Liam Irwin (Mary Immaculate College, Limerick), Br Anthony Keane, Margaret McCoy, Sarah McCrutcheon (archaeologist, Limerick County Council), Mike Maguire (Limerick City Library), Eileen O'Connor, Gregory O'Connor (National Archives, Dublin), Pat Punch, Andrew Potter (Royal Academy Library, London), Arthur Quinlan, Brendan Rooney (National Gallery Ireland), Christopher Thornhill (archivist, Royal Cruising Club), and the staff of de Valera Public Library, Ennis County Clare, the General Register Office, the Irish Co-operative Organisation Society Ltd, Mary Immaculate College, Limerick, The National Archives of Ireland, The National Archives London, Manuscript Department National Library of Ireland, St Mary's Cathedral Archive, Manuscript Department Trinity College Dublin and University of Limerick Special Collections.

Photographs and Illustrations

Most of the photographs and illustrations are from the collections of Gary MacMahon, Murrogh O'Brien Foynes Island and Susan Ruck. The photograph on page 12 is from Trinity College Oxford Archive, College Photograph 1900, courtesy of the President and Fellows of Trinity College Oxford. The cartoons and illustrations on pages 15, 17, 18 and 21 are courtesy the United Arts Club Dublin. The photograph of *Asgard* on page 34 is courtesy of The National Museum of Ireland. Of the remainder every effort has been made to identify the copyright holders. We welcome any information that would help us update our records.

Introduction

Saoirse was the focus of Dun Laoghaire Harbour on the afternoon of 20 June 1923. A modestly sized yacht, she was surrounded by a flotilla of small boats, her decks crowded with people and her sails hoisted. On deck Conor O'Brien, nervous and boisterous, presided over a scene he did not particularly relish.[1] He had decorated the newly painted cabin with oil sketches and now he was handing out drinks, noting the presence of a few press photographers and the absence of certain family members and friends among the noisy well-wishers. Finally, at 4.30 p.m., he was able to clear the ship and, with his crew, prepare to set sail.

Dermod, his older brother, who had been dodging Conor's curses on the yacht, watched from the shore as *Saoirse* slipped away, now elongated and grey against the changing blue of the sea and sky, now dazzlingly white as she was caught by the sun. Later he sat down to write to his wife Mabel: To me it is all a great adventure of Conor's and I admire the spirit which keeps him young enough [he was 42] to start out on it, and I rather loathe the apparent necessity of sending him off with golliwogs and other toys as if he were off for a days summery [cruise] to the Isle of Man.'[2] Next day photographs of *Saoirse*, Conor and his crew featured in the centre pages of *The Irish Times* and the *Irish Independent*: they had embarked on a circumnavigation and expected to be away from home for two years.[3]

Like many extraordinary sailors, Conor wrote. His description of this voyage was a best-seller. His other books – sailing adventure stories for teenagers,

technical books on rigs, deep water sailing and yacht design, accounts of his three yachts and his life in the Mediterranean on board *Saoirse* with his wife in the 1930s – amount to a championing of small yacht sailing. Founded on practicality, independence and passion this activity did not rely on wealth and was in tune with an aspiration shared by many in the early twentieth century.

Although Conor O'Brien has an honoured place in the yachting world he is hardly known beyond it. Even in Ireland he is rarely mentioned, although he was born into a family with many members who have made a significant contribution to Irish life. His grandfather, William Smith O'Brien, was a celebrated nationalist, his aunt, Charlotte Grace O'Brien, was a writer and social reformer, his brother, Dermod O'Brien, a well-known painter. But, until recently, only Smith O'Brien has received any serious attention.[4]

During his lifetime Conor's achievements were recognised, but because there has been no subsequent account of his life they have not been assessed.[5] His life – his Ascendancy background, his English education, his architectural training, his Arts and Crafts sensibility, his mountaineering, his talented and politically responsible family, his failed attempts to find a role in independent Ireland, his marriage to an artist who lived with him on his boat, his love of islands – all had a bearing on his sailing so that it is stamped with his particular, inimitable style. He could be reclusive. He lived physically on the margins of society either in his boat or on Foynes Island, an island in the Shannon Estuary in the west of Ireland. But he was very much a man of the early twentieth century; his ability to shape his life and his particular passions resonated with the concerns of his contemporaries. He also played a role in Irish history: a Protestant Home Ruler and

Pastel portrait of Conor O'Brien by Kitty Clausen, 1927. Conor was 47 early member of Sinn Féin with an interest in the Irish language, he ran guns for the Volunteers in 1914 and had a strong desire to serve Ireland, which he did through the Irish Agricultural Organisation Society (IAOS) and the fisheries and, with many of his contemporaries, by serving in the First and Second World Wars. Sailing to the farthest oceans in boats designed and made in Ireland he may have hoped that his sailing would find a place in the cultural or sporting life, or even the mythology, of the new state. So far it has been all but ignored.

Conor O'Brien, perhaps typically of someone who is largely forgotten, has left a trail that is by turns hopeful and bleak. There is no extensive archive of personal papers. But he does make an appearance in the O'Brien and Childers papers of the National Library of Ireland and Trinity College Dublin. His books are out of print, but still obtainable. The O'Brien family retain Monare, Conor's sister's house on Foynes Island, and a place that was a second home to him. His impressive family home, Cahirmoyle – now a nursing home – and the diminutive house that sheltered him in his last years on Foynes Island still stand and, to a great extent, in the landscapes that O'Brien knew. But his beloved home, the yacht *Saoirse*, was destroyed in a hurricane while helplessly anchored in a Jamaican harbour in 1979. The world in which sailing boats were the conduit for coastal trade had faded by his death in 1952. It has now irrevocably gone. Yet traces remain. An elderly man is currently repairing a 1950s' wooden rowing boat in a garage decorated with paintings of the ketches and schooners of the Shannon Estuary that he made fifty years previously. He had known O'Brien on Foynes Island in the late 1940s. Meanwhile sailing as a leisure activity is pursued with passion in Baltimore, Dublin Harbour and southern Cornwall, all places where O'Brien sailed. Institutions that O'Brien was associated with survive – adapted of

course – into the twenty-first century: the Royal Irish Yacht Club, The Royal Cruising Club, The Climbers' Club, the Irish Agricultural Organisation Society, the Royal Society of Antiquaries of Ireland, the United Arts Club. His architectural legacy is not immediately impressive and most of the creamery buildings he designed have gone, but creameries are now a valued part of the architectural and social heritage of Ireland. His monuments are safe as an integral part of St Mary's Cathedral, Limerick, a place rooted in twelfth-century O'Brien power and entangled with the family ever since.

Appropriately, the process of uncovering O'Brien was instigated by a sailor with a passion for recovering the sailing boats and the life they generated in Irish rivers and coastal waters. Gary MacMahon's interest in Conor O'Brien intensified when, in the late 1980s, he discovered that *Saoirse* was destroyed but that *Ilen*, the boat O'Brien had designed for the Falkland Islands Company in 1926, was still in Port Stanley, afloat and intact. He decided to bring this boat, one of the last remaining Irish-built timber sailing boats, back to Ireland. The venture brought together many people with an interest in Irish maritime history and generated curiosity about the man who had designed and sailed her south. MacMahon's own interest extended to the compilation of an archive on O'Brien; he collected his publications, drawings, photographs, letters relating to the registration and selling of *Saoirse* and a few family letters. The most valuable part of his collection are the photographs of O'Brien's ships and crews, which give a unique insight into the life of an extraordinary Irish sailor in the first half of the twentieth century. Meanwhile, berthed in Old Court on the River Ilen in County Cork, *Ilen* is waiting to be restored. This book is a first attempt to describe, evaluate and illustrate Conor O'Brien's life and to portray something of his extraordinary spirit.

Family portrait taken c. 1890. In the middle are Edward and his second wife, Julia. In the back row are the children

Chapter 1
O'Brien

Conor O'Brien was born into an ascendancy family with roots in Gaelic Ireland. The O'Briens, who had ruled Thomond since the mid-tenth century, were one of the few royal families to have survived the land redistributions of the seventeenth century. In the nineteenth century the family was conscious of its antiquity and many members carried a concomitant sense of responsibility, none more so than Conor's grandfather, William Smith O'Brien, who had allowed nationalist politics to take precedence over class interests. The second son of the wealthy Dromoland O'Briens, he inherited Cahirmoyle in west County Limerick on the death of his mother, trained as a barrister and entered politics. Here he excelled, beginning his career as a Tory MP. His liberal instincts and growing commitment to Irish interests were expressed in the milestones of support for Catholic Emancipation in 1829 and membership of Daniel O'Connell's Repeal Association in 1843, which campaigned for the repeal of the Act of Union. His idealism led him to increasing sympathy with O'Connell's opponents, the Young Irelanders, who were prepared to entertain violence. In July 1848 Smith O'Brien became the reluctant leader of the Young Ireland rebellion. He was convicted of high treason and exiled to Tasmania in 1849. Pardoned in 1854 he returned to Ireland two years later, 24 years before Conor's birth. He died in 1864.

Several members of his family, particularly his mother and one of his sisters, felt shamed by his involvement in radical politics.[1] However, his daughter, Conor's aunt, Charlotte Grace O'Brien, who would look after her father on his return, admired him and drew inspiration from him. She acknowledged that, selfish and impatient – others have described him as arrogant – he was not an easy man to live with. But she celebrated the qualities that had made him an effective politician, and felt it was impossible that one could be both publicly effective and comfortable to live with. In an essay she evoked the picture of a man of 'very high nervous tension', 'capable of [the] highest self sacrifice, of the most massive and masculine sympathies, of honour so pure that his public name has become a symbol in his nation for honour.' 'Was he', she asked, 'therefore perfect? No... those very qualities that raised his public life were a difficulty in his private.'[2]

Charlotte Grace's delineation of the incompatibility of public and private virtue reflected the Victorian differentiation between the public and the private sphere. However, Charlotte Grace herself did not choose between public effectiveness and domestic comfort; she threw her considerable energy into both. Conor too valued both. He cultivated domesticity, though in an unconventional form. He would also make subversive and orthodox public gestures.

As a young man William Smith O'Brien's eldest son, Edward William, Conor's father, restricted himself to the domestic sphere. A man who liked a well-ordered life – he was described as being 'punctilious and punctual almost to excess'[3] – he showed little interest in nationalist politics. William Smith O'Brien had left Cahirmoyle in trust to his wife before joining the rebellion, and on her death in 1861 (three years before Smith O'Brien's death) Edward inherited the estate.[4] It was a premature inheritance, but Edward readily shouldered his new responsibilities. He paid his father £2,000 a year, made the house available for his siblings and was a practical and economical landlord. The Irish education that his father had given him – he had gone to Trinity College Dublin rather than following his father to Trinity College Cambridge – had resulted in an allegiance to the family estate rather than to the wider issues of politics or culture.

Edward William and other family members in the hall at Cahirmoyle.

James Garth Marshall – the father of Julia Marshall, Edward's second wife.

Edward married Mary Spring Rice in 1863. They only had five years together before Mary died on the Riviera. During that time they travelled extensively, especially in Italy and southern France, and had three children: Dermod, Nelly and Mary. As a child and young woman growing up in Mount Trenchard, a large house just outside the village of Foynes, Mary Spring Rice had been a neighbour of Edward's. Her grandfather, Thomas Spring Rice, the first Lord Monteagle, was a liberal unionist politician who served Limerick city and county and had a distinguished career at Westminster, which culminated in his appointment as Chancellor of the Exchequer in 1835.[5] Her father, Stephen Edward, managed the estate with skill in his father's absence. Both Thomas Spring Rice and Stephen took on responsibility for the tenants' welfare during the Famine. They built a school and diverted relief works to the building of a pier at Foynes, built a model farm near Mount Trenchard and assisted those who wished to emigrate. After the Famine they continued to develop the estate and improve the lives of their tenants by bringing the railway to Foynes and and planning the building of a Catholic church in the village. Stephen died in 1865 and his father a year later. Their local legacy was more practical though probably less potent than William Smith O'Brien's.

Marriage to Mary did not encourage Edward to emulate the social conscience of the Spring Rices, though the alliance with this family may have inspired him in later years. Instead, in 1870, two years after his wife's death, he indulged his aesthetic interests and sensibilities by embarking on the rebuilding of Cahirmoyle. He engaged one of the most inventive architects of the day, J. J. McCarthy, (who was also designing the Catholic church in Foynes) to design the new house.[6] It took five years for a Venetian palace dressed in a rich variety of beautifully crafted Irish stone to emerge. From across the fields, smoothly finished blue and white arches shelter in the grey and pink rusticated walls built from limestone quarried at Moig near Shanagolden. Inside it is one of the most elegant houses of the period. It has a tall, colonnaded entrance hall where leaves – classical acanthus and native oak – dogs, boars, servants' and masters' heads adorn the capitals. Mantlepieces

Katharine (Kitty) Jenny, Edward William, Margaret Ernestine and Julia Garth Marshall c. 1905.

The garden at Cahirmoyle with Katharine and Margaret in the grass. In the background are their parents Edward and Julia.

were specially commissioned from what has been described as the many marbles of Ireland – black Ennis limestone, Cork red and Michelstown brown porphyry, Connemara green and Kilkenny black marble. Cahirmoyle was partly a memorial to Mary, reflecting the love of Italian architecture that she had shared with Edward. It was also the project of a man with exacting standards and the wealth to realise them. And it was an engagement with the incipient cultural Irish Revival in which Irish materials and indigenous craftsmanship were enthusiastically used, revived, displayed and celebrated. It was a way of expressing an allegiance to Ireland without getting involved in politics.

Edward married again in 1880. Julia Mary Marshall was a cousin of Mary Spring Rice's. Her father's substantial wealth was based in England – Yorkshire and Lancashire – and she herself had houses in London and Guildford.[7] Edward moved to her London home in Kensington soon after the marriage and Julia's first child, Edward Conor Marshall O'Brien, soon known as Conor, was born there on 3 November 1880.[8] There would be three more children, a son, Aubrey, born 7 June 1882, and

two daughters, Katharine, known as Kitty, born soon after, and Margaret, born in September 1887.

Conor had arrived at the start of the Land War and this now pulled his father, Edward, periodically back to Ireland. Against his wife's wishes, though not without her support – for Julia was an intelligent and sympathetic woman – Edward would become involved as an intermediary between landlords and tenants in the fraught exchanges in Irish estates. At first, though, he was an aggrieved landlord, stringently opposed to the Land League which was set up in October 1879 to co-ordinate a countrywide campaign against landlord abuses such as eviction and high rents. In March 1881, confronted with tenants who refused to pay rents, Edward served out attorney's letters and wrote to Julia: 'The landlords must stand firm and I think most of them will. It is all-important to break the neck of the land league or we shall have it all over again.'[9]

It was war between landlords and tenants. The government played an ambiguous role, but with the 1881 Land Act it did attempt to put the machinery in place for the resolution of conflict. The Act provided for a Land Commission to set

Charlotte Grace O'Brien.

Front (l to r): Charlotte Grace, Nelly, Margaret and Edward William. Back (l to r): Conor, Dermot, Julia, Katharine (Kitty) and Aubrey.

fair rents. It also provided for Land Commission Courts to resolve disputes arising from the tenants' rejection of current rent levels, and to apply the fair rents. By the late summer Edward had become more sympathetic to individual tenants and was disposed to act more liberally. He now appreciated the importance of the Land Commission Courts and wanted to play a part in administering them. By early November 1881 he had been appointed as a commissioner.

His letters reveal that he enjoyed the work. He relished the journeys on rickety vehicles to remote places – he was sent to Donegal. He respected his colleagues and admired their ability to find solutions that minimised compromise on both sides. He was impressed by the Donegal farmers, two of them 'simply magnificent', 'as straight as your northern men, but broader, with great flowing beards and intelligent and truthful countenances. Very intelligent they are to talk to'.[10] He found the rents had been far too high and that reductions were necessary. If he felt anxious or tired he went for recuperative walks in the wild scenery that he loved.

His commitment to the work of the courts is underlined by the fact that he had only been married for a year and, from odd comments in the letters, revealed himself as a man who enjoyed being at home with his wife and family. In July 1880, when problems at Cahirmoyle had first taken him back to Ireland, he wrote to Julia, 'It is very disgusting having to run away from you into all this work.' (9 July 1880, NLI.) When Julia sent him a photograph of baby Conor in December 1881 he replied: 'You have made me very happy dear and not that alone but very comfortable – taken all sorts of anxieties and troubles off my shoulders without I hope transferring them to yours. You suit me so well and are so good to the young ones and make life almost too smooth and easy for me.'[11] In 1884 he wrote a pamphlet on land purchase.[12] The following year he was involved in the framing of the Land Purchase Act (Ashbourne Act) which refined the Land Act of 1881 by increasing loans for purchase to 100 per cent. What was effectively a land revolution would culminate in The Wyndham Act of 1903. Conor, valuing the Ashbourne Act as part of the radical change in land holding that would see vast areas of land transferred to former tenants, would cite his father's work in his bid for a senate seat in 1925.

These were also the years – 1881 to 1883 – in which Charlotte Grace O'Brien did the public work for which she became modestly well known. In the twelve years between the death of Mary and Edward's marriage to Julia, Charlotte Grace, in her twenties, had been like a mother to their three children. A woman who was habitually careless of her appearance and who valued spontaneity over finish, she did not always get on with her ordered and finicky brother.[13] Charlotte was particularly uncomfortable in the new Cahirmoyle which seemed to require a poised and polished mistress. But she loved the children as her own. When they moved to England in 1880 she, 34 and unmarried, was distraught and a little self-pitying. She wrote in a letter to her niece Mary revealing her love for them and her reliance on their love for her:

> I am most glad about your father's marriage, most glad he and Aunt Julia will be happy, and that you should be home again; and yet, do you know, I have felt torn to pieces in the thought of it. There's nothing in the world to me like your love for me, you children, and yet I know how easy it is for young hearts to grow away from those they are not always with. You do not know what suffering it was to me to part with you, and this is in a way the seal of our parting. It will only depend on you now, dear youngs [sic], not to grow away from me entirely. I do not believe anyone, till you marry, will ever love you as I do … you must not let it [the tie between us] go; you have everything before you and I have only my dogs!'[14]

But she was able to turn disappointment into productive work, and in 1881 she began her campaign to improve the treatment of female emigrants who had chosen to leave Ireland at this time. She was an early admirer of Michael Davitt, the founder of the Land League, something that annoyed Edward who belittled her interest as hero-worship.[15] She devised and carried out her own campaign. She lobbied parliament, writing reports about the accommodation and treatment of emigrants on Atlantic steamships, and she criticised government policy that encouraged emigration. In November 1881 she set up a lodging house for emigrant women in Cobh, and installed herself as the lodging's housekeeper. The following autumn she went to America, setting up a refuge in New York for arriving female emigrants. This well-publicised and effective work ceased in 1883 when she returned to Foynes. She was becoming increasingly deaf and became temporarily depressed. But she was not by any means a spent force.

The political involvement of his father and aunt was unlikely to have had a direct influence on the young Conor. But their allegiance to Ireland conveyed in their work and talk, and the differences of opinion, created an atmosphere within the family that Conor no doubt absorbed as he grew up. He spent most of his childhood in London in his mother's house in Roland Gardens. It was a large terraced house off the Old Brompton Road in South Kensington, spacious and comfortable, with the vast bay window, terracotta tiles, pillar-decorated front door and rear mews that were the necessary accoutrements of late Victorian upper middle class houses. It was close to the museums of Exhibition Road, a healthy walk to Hyde Park and the Albert Hall, and not far from the river at Chelsea, all destinations that were no doubt familiar to the young Conor. With his brothers and sisters, he made periodic trips to Julia's family homes in the North of England. They also went to Ireland. In at least two of the stories he wrote for teenagers in his fifties and sixties Conor evoked the complex experience of arriving in Ireland from England as a partial stranger. The two teenage protagonists in *Two Boys Go Sailing* have very different responses to Roaringwater Bay in west Cork, each perhaps reflecting experiences of O'Brien's. One of the boys sees the scores of islands, glittering sea, wild rocky coast and heathery hinterland and pronounces it 'all … poetry and romance', while the other notices the lack of yacht sails and the thin turf smoke rising from the village, and thinks it bleak compared with the bustling seaside resorts he knows in England.

The earliest photograph of Conor O'Brien.

A young Conor O'Brien.

The family often went to Derrynane in Kerry where they stayed in Keating's Hotel, and met the Dunravens, an Anglo-Irish family who lived near Cahirmoyle in Adare Manor in County Limerick and were keen sailors. Conor's intense feeling for the place was expressed in a lyrical passage included in *From Three Yachts*. Here, at the age of 47, he evoked vivid childhood impressions while ostensibly describing his ideal seaside:

> Those virtues must include rocks, for
> without their shelter the coast is an
> inhospitable desert, untenable in a breeze of
> wind. There must be sand, pure white sand,
> that the water over it may shine with an
> emerald gleam between the purple patches
> where it covers weed-grown rocks; and of
> course the water must be clear enough to
> show this. There must be a little beach of
> pebbles … to rattle cheerfully when the
> swell runs in on them; and of course there
> must be from time to time a swell to rattle
> them. High-water mark along the strand

> must be traced out with a line of rare and
> beautiful shells, not with corks and clinkers,
> and low-water mark must be at such a
> distance from it as suits those who care for
> bathing in such a place, and there must be
> no deep and dangerous holes … Therefore,
> let there be rock-pools, out of which you can
> easily climb if you fall into them, and let
> them not be too completely paved with sea-
> urchins, whose spines discourage falling in,
> which is the way to learn swimming.[16]

Sometimes they went to Cahirmoyle. Conor was there with his brother, Aubrey, his half-sister, Mary, and his father in March 1891 when he was ten. It was a sociable and active holiday in which the children got a taste of the free-ranging childhoods that their Anglo-Irish contemporaries were living now that the Land War was over. They went hunting, Conor on his own pony; they visited the Spring Rices at Mount Trenchard; they celebrated St Patrick's Day (Conor's father gave him a watch); and they built 'a house near the quarry garden' which may be the

Ard an Óir, Foynes, built after 1864.

Charlotte Grace O'Brien.

stone structure that resembles a beehive hut that can be seen in a photograph in the family album.[17] This album also contains a studio photograph of Conor as a boy. He is wearing a tweed coat, a shirt and tie, and a cap. He has freckles, narrow eyes and a pleasant, slightly cheeky, happy expression.

It is not far from Cahirmoyle to Foynes, the small village on the Shannon which was being nurtured by the Spring Rices. They had built a pier, set up a sawmill, commissioned J. J. McCarthy to design a church of miniature perfection and given the place the ambiguous distinction of a family cross on the wooded hill overlooking the harbour. Later they would add the decorum of Arts and Crafts cottages to the straggling main street. Although Foynes was a deep and sheltered port and had harboured transatlantic shipping since the early nineteenth century, it was still a quiet place, punctuated by the grocer-cum-public houses then typical of Irish villages, and confined by the steeply wooded hills that rose behind it.

Conor's aunt, Charlotte Grace, now lived at Ard an Óir, the red-brick house she had built on

the gorse-covered hill just outside the village, with her companion Peggy Briscoe. Recovered from her depression, she lived an intense life, inspired in many varied ways by the local life. She filled her terraced garden with carefully positioned pines and laurels and evergreen plants from New Zealand and Australia. She studied native plants, sending her botanical findings to the naturalist, Robert Lloyd Praeger for his *Irish Topographical Botany*. She wrote poetry and novels, many for younger readers. Her first novel, *Light and Shade*, published in 1878, was based on an account of the Fenian rising in Ardagh in 1867 given to her by a leader, carpenter and author, William Upton.[18] The novel reveals an awareness of the radical nationalist past before nationalists were honouring such milestones, and indicates a sympathy with those who had been involved. She converted to Catholicism in the early 1890s.

One of the passions of her last years was the Irish language. She was a friend of Douglas Hyde, the first president of the Gaelic League, an organisation founded in 1893 to revive Irish as a spoken language. He visited Ard an Óir in 1891. In July 1905, 60 and very deaf, she gave a rousing public speech at an open-air Gaelic League rally in nearby Abbeyfeale. Her Gaelic League enthusiasm sparked her niece, Nelly, (38 in 1905) to learn Irish, become a fluent speaker and work for the League, which she did with flair and enthusiasm.

Charlotte Grace had maintained an affectionate friendship with all her nieces and nephews, although nothing has survived which indicates her particular relationship with Conor. She welcomed them to Ard an Óir, and in the 1890s built a house in Foxrock near to her sister Lucy Gwynn to introduce them to Dublin society. Outspoken, opinionated, busy, large and untidy, she made a lasting impression on the next generation. Her nephew Stephen Gwynn, Lucy's son, later a nationalist politician and writer, wrote movingly about her in a memoir, recalling that, free from domestic cares and the criticisms of people like her brother Edward, she was a delightful, light-hearted companion. Most impressively perhaps for Conor was the fact that she lived an unorthodox life, uninhibited by others' opinions, free to pursue her interests and passions. Her rootedness in Foynes – her appreciation of the people who lived and worked there, her love of the place – was also a compelling example for him. She identified with the estuary, wild and unsung as it was, much as he would identify with it. 'That's the place for me; grand', she wrote about the ancient graveyard that stands starkly on the top of the hill behind her house where she wanted to be buried. 'The wind … sweep[s] up from the Atlantic, the sky [is] heavy with broken clouds, the mild air bear[s] uncertain drifts of rain, the river [is] grim and wild, the Fergus desolate and grey, the bogland black, and a big heap of bones at my feet.'[19]

Conor's immediate family was close-knit and affectionate. Edward's letters to Julia, while reserved, reveal a deep bond of trust and affection between them. Edward was informative about what he was doing and gave his opinions in a direct manner, confident of Julia's interest and concern. He often thought about the children, asking her to kiss them for him, or telling her how much he liked their letters, whatever they had to say.[20]

Julia was more forthcoming about her feelings for Edward, particularly her anxiety if he failed to write. She also sought to empathise with his experiences. On 28 November 1900 she told him that just to know where he was and what his conditions were would be valuable 'so that anything you tell would have meaning for me.' Unlike many of her peers she was an involved mother. She often took the children away with her to spend part of the winter in Switzerland and the summer in Italy. Her letters to Edward were full of news about their activities, her concern for their health and her involvement in their education.

When it came to decisions about careers the letters reveal that the father and mother discussed the issues together, although Edward made the final decisions. In 1902, when Conor was 22, the question arose whether he should inherit Cahirmoyle. Edward was ill (he had a protracted illness before his death) and Dermod, the eldest son, had embarked on a career as an artist. He had little interest in the estate with its considerable problems and expense. Julia had strong opinions but was careful to adopt a conciliatory tone.

> *I need not say that anything you may decide on to make D's position securer will be entirely approved of by me. I do not like to put myself in the place of providence as you know & it was a strong measure for me to express such a decided opinion as I did about the undesirability of hanging up Conor with Cahirmoyle, considering that he has not the qualities for it as D has. I shall go along with anything you find right to do, you know I have the greatest wish to make D free to live his life & make the most of himself'.[21]*

She was, significantly, arguing against her son inheriting the estate. She understood the needs of her children, and their happiness was her priority.

The boys received a good formal English education that was not available to the girls. Conor was sent as a scholar to Winchester College in September 1894 at 13. He left in the summer of 1899 at 18, without any prizes but with a good academic record. Apart from being clever and hard working,

Conor O'Brien in his teens.

he rowed and at 15 he was the cox of a four of junior scholars.[22]

He went straight from Winchester to Trinity College Oxford. In a college photograph taken in the summer of 1900, the final term of his first year, Conor is one of the few dressed in an elegant, light jacket. He is also one of the few without a straw boater. But he stands out from his contemporaries by the way he looks directly at the camera. Around him the young men look anxious, diffident, dreamy, speculative, while Conor appears direct and confident, someone prepared to stand up for himself. He spent four years at Trinity taking a fourth-class degree in Natural Science (Chemistry) in the summer of 1903, a result that suggests his heart was not in his work. There are no records that he sailed, rowed or climbed for the college or the university.[23] In his final year he was a member of an Irish debating society, St Patrick's Club. It had been founded the previous year by, among others, Lady Gregory's son, Robert.[24] He was a unionist with a growing interest in Irish culture, and a friend of W. B. Yeats. Thomas Aubrey Spring Rice, a cousin of Conor's and the heir to Mount Trenchard, was also a member. The club was purposefully non-political; when it debated compulsory land purchase

it refrained from voting. In Conor's last term, Robert Gregory read a paper on Irish journalism in which he argued the Irish Literary Revival line that commercialism had not lowered standards as much in Ireland as in England. Thus Conor was presented with Irish issues in a tentatively reformist atmosphere.

During the vacations Conor read and worked, inspiring his sisters – particularly Kitty, who was bookish and not at all eager for the social distractions available to her – to emulate him. While he read logic and Greek plays in the Swiss Alps Kitty, encouraged by her father, was studying his logic books and asking for algebra lessons.[25] Both girls studied French and Italian. When Nelly expressed an interest in Arabic, Julia arranged for vacation tuition at Oxford. The girls would develop their artistic talents, particulary music, encouraged by their mother who was a good pianist. Kitty learnt to play the cello, Margaret studied violin and viola; they would play into their adult lives for their own amusement at home and in orchestras. Nelly enjoyed painting; she would later train at the Slade School of Art. They were good companions for Conor who would remain close to and in many ways dependent on his sisters throughout his life, calling on them intermittently for their support, for practical help and for congenial company.

Conor and his sisters also enjoyed sport. During their adolescence and early twenties they skied and tobogganed in their Alpine retreats, and Julia took them walking in the mountains.[26] Conor tobogganed down icy slopes that no one else would attempt. He seems to have been slow to take a focused interest in strenuous outdoor activity, but this lengthy period of outdoor fun with his sisters cemented their relationship. Although girls make rare appearances in his later stories, they are treated generously. In *Two Boys Go Sailing* Podge is as agile and daring as the boys. There are differences. She is more confident and sensible than the boys, though less well equipped, and able, with her greater understanding of people, to manipulate them. When she is climbing with Foxy she counters his declaration that 'girls can't hang on by their hands' with the assertion that they have better balance;

'Truly, thought Foxy', a few minutes later when she has climbed the almost impossible, 'girls have the better balance'.[27]

Conor and his sisters were close to Dermod, Nelly and Mary who got on well with their stepmother. Lennox Robinson in his biography of Dermod records that Julia's letters to Dermod were consistently loving, and that Dermod relied on her for sympathy, particularly during his father's long illness. There was some replication of his father's relationship with Julia, for sympathy and understanding overrode very different styles: Dermod was meticulous and immaculate like Edward, whereas Julia was informal and casual, a wearer, sometimes, of cotton flannel skirts without petticoats, much to Dermod's dismay.[28]

When Conor and his sisters were young their half-brother and half-sisters must have felt like aunts and uncles: Dermod was fifteen years older than Conor; he went to Cambridge when Conor was three and began travelling in Europe (he trained at Antwerp Royal Academy of Fine Arts) when Conor was seven. An avuncular letter from Dermod to Julia's children written in August 1888 (when Dermod was 23 and Conor 8) has survived.[29] Written from Limerick it begins, 'My dear children', and tells them about his journey to Ireland, their uncle Lucius (then rector in Adare), and his meeting with Michael Davitt. Most surprisingly, it gives news of crops: 'prices of stock and butter pretty high & hay being well saved & in abundance', suggesting that their father's concerns were household issues. He signed himself 'W. Dermod O'Brien'. This was less distancing than it looks today for the O'Brien siblings often signed their letters to each other with their full names.

Such letters encouraged the younger children to write, and it was to Dermod that the ten-year-old Conor reported on his holiday activities at Cahirmoyle, the place in which Dermod had spent his childhood. They were not regular correspondents and a letter from December 1901 in which Conor congratulated Dermod on his engagement reveals that Dermod had sent a dutiful birthday letter and that his more flippant, self-absorbed younger

Conor O'Brien (right)

brother had omitted to reply. When he was older, Conor had an empathy with young boys and occasionally looked after a vulnerable boy, training him to sail: they may have benefited from Dermod's care with his younger brother.

In his early twenties Conor developed an interest in stained glass and Irish antiquities, largely though not entirely independently of both his family and Oxford. In a letter to Dermod written in December 1901 during his third year at Oxford, the 21-year-old Conor displayed a confident knowledge of the history and technique of stained-glass design, and was able to advise Dermod about colours and framing. In 1902, now in his last year at Oxford, Conor joined the Royal Society of Antiquaries of Ireland. He was proposed by George James Hewson, a fellow of the society, and Conor's membership is recorded in the journal for 1902. A vigorous antiquarian society that had been set up in the mid-nineteenth century to promote the recording and preserving of ancient and medieval monuments as well as knowledge of Irish customs and language, it produced a scholarly annual journal that encompassed ogham stones, medieval churches, iron age brooches and seventeenth-century travellers' diaries. Conor's uncles, Lucius and Robert Vere, were already members.

When Edward and Julia discussed Conor's

Yachting in Derrynane at the turn of the twentieth century.

career in the summer of 1902 (after his third year at Oxford) it was clear that Conor wanted to be an architect. Fifteen years previously when Dermod had been writing to his father about his desire to be a painter, Edward, cautious about the financial rewards of an artistic career, had suggested architecture, though without much enthusiasm.

> The only other profession that occurs to me is architecture. *It is not a good profession, but it is one that would I think suit you and in which you could reckon on earning something.*
>
> *Willie tells me that in architecture you may consider you do well if you can earn £100 a year by the end of four years. I presume you might be well satisfied if you could earn as much at painting by that time.*[30]

Dermod did train as a painter, and by 1902 had some, though limited, success. Edward now had no qualms about architecture. The same architect friend,

Willie, now recommended that they approach John Thomas Micklethwaite, a well-established Gothic Revival and conservation architect who had been appointed surveyor to Westminster Abbey in 1898, and had written on architectural history; 'the best authority on old churches in England', Julia was told.[31] He was an obvious choice for a young man with an interest in architectural history.

It is not known whether Conor was apprenticed to Micklethwaite or how he was supported financially. Edward had told Dermod in 1887 to expect a small allowance for his training which may extend to the rest of his life, and he may have provided the same for Conor. In one of his later books Conor gives a glimpse of his wayward student self, drawn to the motion of nearby windmills when he was sent to measure and admire an ancient church in Lincolnshire. 'No one could hold a tape to that; it was very much alive', he wrote of the magnificent eight-armed windmill.[32]

Trinity College, Oxford, summer 1900. Conor O'Brien, who was just nearing the end of his first year, is standing sixth

Chapter 2
Architect, Mountaineer
& Young Man in Dublin

Once he started his training in an architectural office in 1903, Conor began to go more frequently to Ireland.[1] Dermod no doubt was an influence. Success had eluded him in London, so Dermod had moved to Ireland, and by late 1901 he had bought a house in Mountjoy Square with his sister, Nelly. Conor was interested in historic buildings in Ireland, especially the picturesque, ruined castles and friaries associated with the O'Brien family in Limerick and Clare. In 1905 he was drawing and measuring the ruins of Askeaton Castle and Franciscan Friary, and the friaries in Ennis and Quin, an ambitious undertaking for many of the ruins were dangerous, particularly Askeaton Castle, whose main tower rises majestically and precariously over its small town.[2]

One of Conor's first architectural commissions was to design the reredos (the screen erected behind an altar) on the east wall of the sanctuary in St Mary's Cathedral in Limerick. His uncle Lucius O'Brien was now the Dean, and the O'Brien family were paying for the work. An O'Brien ancestor, King Domnall Mór Ua Briain was credited with founding the cathedral in the late twelfth century. The austere, arcaded nave and sanctuary of that building still lay at the heart of the church, although it was now comfortably roofed with a Victorian timber vault. In the medieval period the side walls of the aisles had been punctured by arches, and a series of chapels built beyond, extending the building laterally, while outside a distinctive crenellated tower allowed the cathedral to dominate the city. In the nineteenth century there had been two ecclesiologically inspired restorations, the most lasting element being the redesign of the windows that were filled

with brilliantly coloured, iconographic stained glass. The O'Brien presence was concentrated in the sanctuary. Domnall Mór's vast late twelfth-century tomb slab, decorated with sinuous animal carvings, had been placed there by Lucius. He had put it below an early seventeenth-century wall monument to Donough O'Brien, the Fourth Earl of Thomond and his wife: two stiff, recumbent figures dwarfed by the renaissance architecture that was then new to Ireland.[3]

By May 1906 the Dean had £500 in subscriptions from Conor's father, Conor's uncles Robert Vere and Donough O'Brien (all brothers of the Dean, the latter an architect) and Lord Inchiquin who headed the senior branch of the family and lived in Dromoland Castle. It was in May that Lucius asked his young and possibly not yet qualified nephew to do the designs.[4] Conor, based in the family house in Guildford, took on the job with a mixture of confidence and apprehension.[5] He was afraid to give his opinions to the Dean (Conor thought paint as good as mosaic for the proposed central panel) but promptly produced finished drawings for estimates and presentation to the subscribers. He expressed his anxieties to Dermod, who was to design the mosaic figures. He also put pressure on Dermod indirectly, through Nelly, to complete his designs and act as a go-between: 'He seems very anxious that you should get the designs for the mosaics done and push it through with the authorities', Nelly wrote later to Dermod.[6]

The stone screen and central panel, a rather laborious exercise in Gothic arcading lightened with carved plaques that extends across the wall

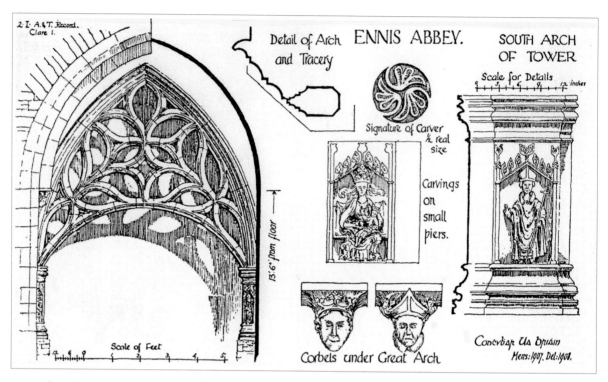

Extract from Conor's article on Dromcliff parish, County Clare, in *The Architectural and Topographical Record*, June 1908.

behind the high altar, was erected in June 1907.[7] It came alive when Dermod's delightful red, gold and blue mosaic triptych figures were added to the panel directly behind the altar in 1911.[8] It is now the gleaming focus of the sanctuary, a lighter, early twentieth-century touch beside the bluntness of the ancient slab and stylistic hesitations of the renaissance tomb.

At the time Conor was working on St Mary's reredos he had become involved in the conservation movement in England. One of the characteristics of nineteenth-century ecclesiastical restoration had been the destruction of post- or late medieval work, and rebuilding in earlier styles. William Morris and his followers such as the architect W. R. Lethaby, who were vehemently opposed to the destruction of all old and particularly original fabric, called for the study of existing ecclesiastical buildings. Morris established the Society for the Study of Ancient Buildings, and in 1908 The Architectural and Topographical Society was formed specifically to

record the design and condition of ancient buildings. Conor O'Brien, who was a founder member, sat on the executive committee.

This work brought him into contact with the Arts and Crafts establishment in England; Lethaby, and the architects Mervyn Macartney and Edward Prior were on the Advisory Council of the society. These three, involved in design as well as architecture, had set up the Art Workers' Guild, which stressed the equal status of all branches of design. This was one of many design groups that flourished in the early twentieth century, exhibiting at the annual Arts and Crafts Exhibition shows. An Arts and Crafts Exhibition Society was founded in Ireland in 1894, and there were Irish studios such as the Dun Emer Guild (fabrics), Cuala Press (books) and An Túr Gloine (stained glass), which designed and made objects according to Arts and Crafts principles. The emphasis was on handworking, the use of high-quality, indigenous materials, and utility. The architect Richard Orpen, who had helped to

Arts Club cartoon by Beatrice Elvery commemorating a party given to welcome Sir William Orpen as a member entitled 'The members of the Arts Club aiming at immortality procure a painter and proceed to pose for their portraits'. Back (l to r): Page Dickinson, Alan Duncan, J. M. Hone, Mervyn Columb, Count Casimir Markievicz, W. B. Yeats. Middle (l to r): Frank Craig, Frank Sparrow, Dominick Spring Rice, Beatrice Campbell, George Woods, Sir John O'Connell. Front (l to r): Betty Duncan, Jim Duncan, Conor O'Brien, Sir William Orpen, Richard Orpen.

restore Dermod's house in Mountjoy Square and who would work with Conor in the 1920s, was an enthusiastic member of the Irish Arts and Crafts Society. It is more than likely that Conor, who would later espouse Arts and Crafts principles in his yacht design (though without naming them as such), attended exhibitions and visited studios in Ireland and England at this time, absorbing the ethos.

Conor used his measured drawings of Askeaton, Quin and Ennis as a basis for three articles for the Architectural and Topographical Society journal.[9]

It was work of extremely high quality.[10] He presented sheets of meticulous, measured drawings using a variety of line weights, laid out in an attractive and easily readable style. These sheets were intermixed with more impressionistic views of the ruins in their overgrown settings. Careful, authoritative, clear and exhaustive, these drawings convey an interest in all the details of construction and style, and an ability to present them with economy. It is clear that O'Brien could have had a career as an architectural historian in the mould of Harold Leask, who wrote several influential books on early Irish architecture filled with similar drawings and worked for the government as an adviser.

However, such careers are extremely difficult to construct and Conor needed to earn his living. Despite his obvious enthusiasm for antiquarian and historical work, he must have had a suspicion, even a realisation, that he would not be able to sustain it and he does not seem to have pursued the work further. Instead he became the Irish Agricultural Organisation Society (IAOS) architect for creameries in County Limerick.

It is probable that this job came to him through Dermod who had become a member of the Irish Agricultural Organisation Society committee in March 1904, and a director of the Irish Agricultural Wholesale Society in 1906. These were both part of Irish co-operation, a movement that had been associated with Conor's family and near neighbours since its inception. Horace Plunkett had first publicly explored his ideas about economic self-help and combination at a meeting in September 1889 on the estate of his friend Lord Monteagle. Monteagle and Edward O'Brien had been among the first to set up co-operative creameries – Edward O'Brien had helped set up the Ardagh Creamery in 1891. In 1894 the IAOS had been formally established to provide a co-operative economic framework for tenants and farmers and to co-ordinate existing co-operatives. Like the Gaelic League, co-operation was a popular movement that promoted self-sufficiency. Non-political, at least initially, the organisations attracted both unionists and nationalists. Working in tandem with the land revolution, in which Edward O'Brien had played a role, the co-operative movement worked outside the political arena to improve standards of living for large numbers of people.

Dermod approached self-help from a unionist perspective, hoping that peaceful improvement would circumvent the need for political change. Conor had nationalist leanings, joining Arthur Griffith's Sinn Féin after it was founded in 1905.[11] Although less radical at this period than it would become after the 1916 Rising Sinn Féin did aim at political separation (though under an English crown), proposing passive resistance to the existing

system and the forming of a national assembly in the interim. Self-help was an underlying principle, with an emphasis on the development of Irish industry behind high protective tariffs. At this time Sinn Féin was a broad church, and Conor was no doubt unaware of groups (such as the Irish Republican Brotherhood) that used Sinn Féin as a respectable front for their more radical separatist ambitions. Whatever his particular political beliefs, Conor's work designing creameries for the IAOS was a practical contribution to an aspect of the self-help movement which was particularly successful at this period, for co-operative creameries producing butter were being constructed in towns and villages all over Ireland.

By March 1909 Conor was an official IAOS architect for creamery buildings with an office in the headquarters at Plunkett House in Merrion Square, Dublin.[12] Here he worked with a team which included James Fant, the creamery inspector, and Mr Riddall, the organiser for the IAOS.

The surviving memos and letters reveal that Conor was a knowledgeable and diligent architect. This did not rule out an informal element to his practice. He brought his work to various family houses in west Limerick – in November 1912 he was writing from Mount Trenchard – and employed his sister Margaret as his secretary.[13] He allowed humour to creep into his correspondence: 'Unless someone has been bewitching the plans …' he wrote of the plans for Bruree Creamery. He might also disappear for longer than agreed. A courteously irate letter was sent to Snowdonia in April 1912 where he was climbing, telling him that Mr Fant wanted to consult him urgently.

Creamery buildings – dairies, well houses, engine rooms, managers' houses – were simple, utilitarian structures, and by the 1900s were roughly standardised. Conor had a number of designs which he pulled out and modified for different jobs: Drombana Co-operative Creamery, for example, was built to the same design as Bruree, which, with different windows, was based on Coleman's Well.[14] The buildings were a pragmatic mix of old and new materials and technologies: traditional slates for the roofs, nineteenth-century-

Cartoon by Beatrice Elvery for the United Arts Club, 'In the good old times before the licence. Members arriving for a House Dinner, 1910.' (Selected figures l to r): George Woods (holding a bottle), Count Casimir Markievicz (with pistol), Page Dickinson (holding his coat), Conor O'Brien (with a bottle), J. M. Hone, Dominick Spring Rice (hat in hand).

style timber sash windows, concrete for the walls, steps and thresholds. Conor also prepared specifications for the machinery and fittings. Like many architects he had an interest in the way things worked.

It was a comfortable, undemanding niche, providing a regular supply of work and a steady income. It was not a job that someone of Conor's restlessness and independence would keep for long. It is perhaps surprising that he lasted as long as he did.

Julia died in 1907, Edward in 1909. Nelly looked after her father following Julia's death. Dermod had inherited Cahirmoyle before Edward's death. He was a reluctant landlord and far preferred his Dublin life of painting and committees. Relying

on private portrait commissions for an income, he based his studio in the city (he also painted landscapes, mostly for his own satisfaction) and was soon established, becoming president of the Royal Hibernian Academy in 1910. He loved committees and was an enthusiastic member of several national committees. But he could not sever himself from Limerick for Mabel, his wife, had taken to the country life at Cahirmoyle where she was developing the dairy.

In his will Edward bequeathed most of the rest of his possessions to Dermod: his two English houses, furniture and household effects, and income from funds in his marriage settlement.[15] Conor, Aubrey, Kitty and Margaret (there was no mention of Nelly who had inherited Ard an Óir

'To Dance and Dine', one of a pair of pen-and-ink drawings for the Arts Club Christmas dinner and dance, 1931, by Brigid O'Brien, caricaturing members. Conor O'Brien is on the left, holding a model boat. On his right is W. B. Yeats, followed by George Bernard Shaw, Padraic Colum, Lennox Robinson and George Russell. On O'Brien's left is Mrs Kennedy Cahill, followed by Richard Orpen and Sara Allgood (actor). In the air are Sophie Pearce and Mrs Williams (commercial aviator).

eye to status-endowing style that he chose Upper Mount Street, just off Merrion Square, in the middle of fashionable Georgian Dublin, a more desirable address than Mountjoy Square. His relative Denis Gwynn embroidered the picture of a dandyish O'Brien in an article for the *Cork Examiner* in 1961, describing the eighteenth-century-inspired evening dress he wore at this period: plum-coloured dinner jacket, velvet knee breeches, stockings which showed off his legs and knitted garters tied neatly below the knees.[16] Dressy and eccentric, Conor had thrown himself into an ebullient and extrovert Dublin social scene with as much verve as he would later put into his more lonely pursuits.

He met his match for enthusiasm and eccentricity in the United Arts Club, a convivial, high-spirited, non-sectarian, non-political social club. It was founded by Ellie Duncan, the curator of the Municipal Gallery, and her husband James, a civil servant. Conor was a founder member and the club architect. Here he met the exuberant Markieviczs – Constance and Casimir – both painting, both, in the early years of the club, part of the viceregal circle. He also met the poet and later rebel Joseph Mary Plunkett, the omnipresent Oliver St John Gogarty, and W. B. Yeats who, generously and self-indulgently eloquent, effortlessly dominated his contemporaries. Dermod, and Conor's cousin, Mary Spring Rice, were also members. Between 1910 and about 1914 the club was the centre of artistic Dublin, though it maintained a significant presence after the First World War and is still flourishing.

There is a striking innocence about their pre-war fun, centred on impromptu verses and cartoons satirising topical issues or poking fun at themselves. Conor was often in the middle of these high jinks either as author or butt.[17] In Beatrice Elvery's cartoon 'The opening ceremony of the new premises of the United Arts Club, 7 December 1910' (see p. 21), he is a smiling figure in conventional evening dress, smoking a pipe, while the sign on the chair nailed together from odd bits of wood that Beatrice sits on reads, 'Furniture Designed and Executed by Conor O'Brien.' In another Elvery cartoon (see p. 17), 'In the good old times before the licence. Members arriving for a House Dinner, 1910',

from Charlotte Grace, and no mention of Mary who may have been married by then) all got equal shares of money and of estate that was not disposed of to Dermod. Conor now had capital, though not enough to give him an independent income.

He bought a house in Upper Mount Street with his sisters, which he furnished with items from his father's houses. He told Dermod that he did not really want the 'decent' furniture, but 'an architect must keep up some style'. It was no doubt with an

Conor is shown standing with the architect Page Dickinson, two small dapper figures holding bottles of beer, having been admitted by the towering bulk of Casimir Markievicz. The cartoon, 'The members of the Arts Club aiming at immortality procure a painter and proceed to pose for their portraits' (see p. 15), commemorated the party given to welcome the painter William Orpen as a member in 1908. Beatrice laughed affectionately at her fellow members with a few telling details: Conor, by then an enthusiastic sailor, is an overgrown schoolboy squashed into a toy boat, smoking a pipe.

In the aftermath of the rejection of Hugh Lane's gallery by Dublin Corporation in 1913 Conor wrote a revue in which club members such as the architect Frank Sparrow who had been involved in the fiasco took part to comic effect.[18] A more spontaneous joke played by Conor and Dickinson failed to amuse members. Hanging the first exhibition of post-Impressionist paintings seen in Dublin and inspired by their loose style, O'Brien and Dickinson produced twelve versions of their own which fooled most of the audience and for which they had to apologise.

Membership of the Arts Club brought O'Brien into contact with the Irish Literary Revival for Lady Gregory and George Russell, as well as W. B. Yeats, were members. The early years of the club coincided with the ebullient first years of the Abbey Theatre in which Yeats and Gregory were delighting modern audiences with plays rooted in Irish literary traditions, and challenging nationalists' tendencies towards censorship, most notably with the performances of J. M. Synge's *Playboy of the Western World* in 1907. George Russell, the quietly authoritative and slightly paradoxical painter, poet, mystic and editor of the IAOS paper, *Irish Homestead,* bridged the gap between Conor's workaday IAOS world and the literary, artistic world of the club. Conor's literary efforts at this time were confined to Arts Club fun, but the Revival formed a background to his life. Another expression of the desire to establish Irish credentials on a European stage beyond the hegemony of Britain, and another form of self-help, it made Dublin a lively and deeply attractive alternative to London. It was the capital of a country with which Conor increasingly identified.

Conor became a supporter of the revival of Irish as a spoken language. In the summer of 1907 he and his sister Nelly, an enthusiastic, practical woman, taught themselves from the Gaelic League textbook, Eugene O'Growney's *Simple Lessons in Irish*.[19] Nelly joined the Gaelic League in 1910 at the age of 43 and then, emulating the energy and initiative of her aunt, Charlotte Grace O'Brien, began to organise new ventures. She founded the Branch of the Five Provinces in Dublin in 1911. The following year, with money raised through concerts, ceilís, public lectures and donations, she bought the redundant coastguard station in Carrigaholt, County Clare and set up an Irish college.[20] During the war she took a travelling Gaelic League exhibition to America where she had the appeal of an Irishwoman with 'an ancestral halo that glows with such names as Brian Boru … and William Smith O'Brien'.[21] She was irritated at being 'a peg to hang ancestors on', but was not above exploiting her power and enjoying the result: 'We have been trotting out my ancestors & relations in the most shameless way', she wrote to Douglas Hyde in 1915.[22] Little evidence for Conor's interest in Irish has survived for he wrote in English for English audiences and was not active in the Gaelic League. However, in 1908 he signed his *Architectural and Topographical Record* articles Conchubhar Ua Briain and later in life he made a comprehensive list of fish in Irish.[23]

One of Conor's closest friends at this time, Page Dickinson, helped Conor to define his Irish cultural interests. Conor and Dickinson were both outspoken and shared a *joie de vivre*. Dickinson, a year younger than Conor, was a more ambitious architect and ran an architectural practice with Richard Orpen. He cultivated an interest in architectural history. In the face of Irish Revival orthodoxy, which stressed the Irishness of Irish art, Dickinson and O'Brien both argued that Irish Romanesque and Gothic architecture were heavily influenced by Britain. Conor gave a paper on the subject to the Architectural Association of Ireland in March 1912, which went down very badly. Afterwards, the report in the *Irish Builder* gave more

£217,247

Photograph taken at Gorphwysfa, Pen-y-pass in Wales, Easter 1913. Standing (l to r): Geoffrey Winthrop Young, Lloyd Baker, Geoffrey Keynes, Geoffrey Madan, Mrs Slingsby, Cecil Slingsby and George Mallory; seated on the wall (l to r): Robert Mühlberg, Conor O'Brien, Eleanor Slingsby and Hugh Herbert Percy.

space to comments from the floor arguing about the distinctiveness of Irish architecture than to O'Brien's talk.[24] However, where Dickinson valued Georgian architecture above all other styles, particularly in Ireland, Conor would have a lifelong love of the idiosyncrasies of Gothic design wherever he found it. Dickinson despised the Gaelic League and was very damning about it in his 1929 memoir of the period, *The Dublin of Yesterday*: 'The movement was about as logical and as useful as one concerned with teaching people in Devon today the Saxon tongue of pre-Norman days would be'.

Their friendship was most securely held together by their shared enthusiasm for mountain climbing. In the early years – 1909, 1910, 1911 – weekends and holidays were spent climbing the mountains of Ireland with a group from the Arts Club. Later the friends joined the radical, ambitious group of climbers in Snowdonia out of which George Mallory, one of the first British climbers to attempt Mount Everest, would emerge. Although

the British had been attempting challenging rock climbs in the Alps since the mid-nineteenth century it was only at the end of the century that people had begun to climb without guides. This opened up the sport to those without the money to pay for guides and introduced a new set of values: self-reliance and a celebration of the physical and aesthetic experience of climbing. The early guideless climbers of the 1870s had been dismissed as amateurs, but when Geoffrey Winthrop Young, a supremely accomplished climber with a strong social instinct who had been climbing in Wales since the turn of the century, encouraged young mountaineers to stay at remote Gorphwysfa, an inn at Pen-y-pass in Snowdonia, British guideless climbing gained an irresistible focus.

This was cemented in 1909 when Young met George Mallory. Mallory, who had taught himself toughness as a child by sleeping under a single blanket, was a climber of technical brilliance and an almost reckless daring. His combination of athletic body and delicate features made him extremely attractive to Edwardian sensibilities, particularly Bloomsbury homosexuals such as Lytton Strachey who raved 'Mon dieu – George Mallory!' But Mallory, who earned his living as a teacher at Charterhouse public school, seemed immune to admiration: the unselfconsciously brilliant star to which lesser stars gravitated. It was on his third expedition to Mount Everest in 1924 that he and Andrew Irvine died. It is still not known definitively whether they had been to the top when they were last sighted on the north-east ridge and were thus the first men to reach the summit of the earth's highest mountain.[25]

O'Brien may have become involved in climbing through a Winchester connection, Robert Irving. He had been a fellow scholar in 1894–96, and they had shared scholars' accommodation. Irving had returned to the school as a tutor in 1900 and had taken boys, including George Mallory, to the Alps.[26] Another contact was Frank Sparrow from the Dublin Arts Club who was climbing from 1907 in Wales. By the time O'Brien joined the Pen-y-pass climbers at Easter 1911 he had, perhaps inevitably, developed his own personal style. In a photograph

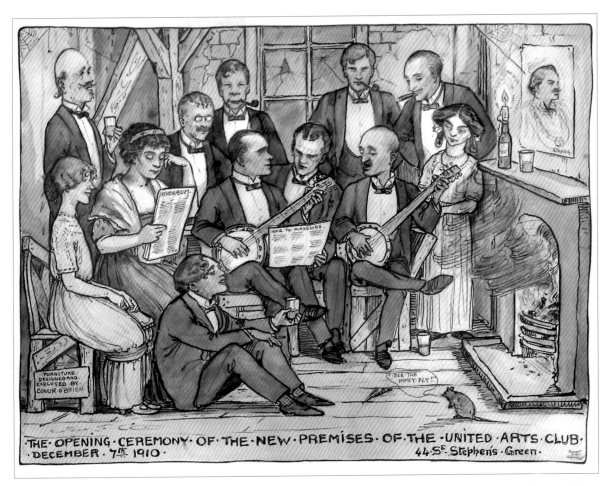

Cartoon by Beatrice Elvery, 'The opening ceremony of the new premises of the United Arts Club, 7 December 1910'. Standing (l to r): C. J. McCarthy, George Woods, Conor O'Brien, Frank Craig, Cyril Dickinson, Betty Duncan; seated (l to r): Beatrice Elvery, Ellie Duncan, Frank Sparrow (with banjo), Page Dickinson, Jim Duncan (also with banjo); sitting on floor: Maurice Joy; photo above fireplace: Dermod O'Brien.

taken at Easter 1913 O'Brien displays subtle sartorial differences from most of the other men: a scarf instead of a tie, no waistcoat. More dramatically he was renowned for climbing in bare feet with a pipe in his mouth. We get an insight into the way he promoted Irishness at this time: the Irish form of his name and his descent from the earls of Thomond was known and he was not above wearing a crottle-dyed homespun suit. A Pen-y-pass couplet sums this up:

Red as a rose the clothes he wore,
His secret name was Conchubor.[27]

Gorphwysfa, like the United Arts Club, encouraged impromptu exhibitionism. In both groups women socialised and performed equally with men, but at Pen-y-pass there were also children who, congregating together, mocked their elders and contributed to the high-spirited atmosphere.[28] There were outhouses called shacks where climbers had communal baths before dinner, and then there were long sessions around the smoking-room fire where they entertained each other with stories, songs, rhymes and verses composed during the climbs. Some evenings there were gymnastics in the hall. December 1911 'set a record for talent', Young recorded in the visitors' book. The weather that time was glorious. They explored the challenging precipice, Lliwedd, under clear skies, encountering an occasional sharp ray of sun that found its way between the rocks. From a distance these figures in sweaters could be seen swinging and turning on ropes, haloed in frost and occasional falls of ice.

Conor was at another large, celebrated meeting in April 1913 that included Geoffrey Young, Mallory, and the Irishman John Todhunter.[29] They sang folk songs, threw snowballs and climbed in blizzard conditions. At another formidable gathering in the spring of 1914, Conor and his sister Kitty met the writer Robert Graves, who had just left school. Graves depicted Conor, in his autobiography *Goodbye To All That*, as a nervous man braced by his robust sister. 'Conor climbed, he told us, principally as a corrective to bad nerves. He would get very excited when any slight hitch occurred; his voice usually rose to a scream. Kitty used to chide him: "Ach, Conor, dear, have a bit of wit!" and Conor would apologize.'[30] Graves was mesmerised by Conor's ability to climb in bare feet. He, like others, explained it by the fact that Conor was a sailor, but he was sceptical about the benefits: 'Often in climbing one has to support the entire weight of one's body on a couple of toes – but toes in stiff boots. Conor claimed that he could force his naked toes farther into crevices than a boot would go.'

Conor was dedicated to the cause of climbing in bare feet. Foxy, the teenage hero of *The Runaways*, a barefoot climber, out-performs his friend on heather-covered rock: 'he could get some support by gripping the heather with his toes, and he could feel under it for hidden steps.' The climax of the story is Foxy's escape out of a narrow Scottish gully. He is standing on a tiny platform initially convinced he will have to wait to be rescued. However, provoked by a pursuer, he manages to put his right foot on a little bracket of rock across a gap. 'His hands were now at the level of the ledge, but he could not let go of the hold he had, because his body was out of balance on one foot only; he would have fallen outward, not across the gap. He felt on the wall behind him with his left toes, and they went into a square-cut slot just wide enough to jam them; it was going to

be a painful business using that as an anchorage, but he could not have used it at all in boots.'

Young, Mallory, O'Brien and others met when they could at Pen-y-pass during the First World War. In December 1915 Mallory (who had been a gunner lieutenant), Herbert Reade and Conor were there in cold, wet weather which did not prevent them attempting a new climb on the west face where, near the top, they were confronted with an overhanging wall, a challenge they all enjoyed. After the war, at Easter 1919, 28 people, including Conor and Kitty, reassembled in perfect weather at Pen-y-pass to try to revive the pre-war spirit of inventiveness and resourcefulness, for several members had died and Geoffrey Winthrop Young had lost a leg.

Young, writing later about these climbs, chartered and celebrated the pre-war optimism and enthusiasm. The songs and stories were, he wrote, not preserved:

> The spirit of confident youth and hope
> decided that there must and would be
> always new ones. And yet how few of that
> gifted youthful band of mountaineers and
> ingenious minds remained long with us. By
> accident, by the chances of life, but chiefly in
> the war – for the young mountaineers were
> the first to volunteer, the first to fall –
> the large majority became themselves only
> bright memories. Athletes and scholars, men
> of many facets, they would have formed a
> remarkable collection in any age; typifying
> even in their unlikeness to each other, the
> many and varied forms of a beauty, in
> appearance and motion, which often among
> human beings forms the accordant setting
> for greatness in thought or of personality.'[31]

The climbers had a formal focus for setting standards and defining a group mentality in The Climbers' Club of which Young was the president for a time. It published a regular journal and Conor wrote two articles for it in 1912 and 1913 in which he displayed his own love of challenges and desire to experiment. 'By our ambition the face of Lliwedd is seamed with thirty routes and their proper variations – an unworthy aim, perhaps, but when I stand in front of the crags I also fall to scheming out Route Thirty-one …'.[32] But his purpose in writing was to make a case for Irish climbing.

He was initially influenced by Page Dickinson. In a joint article published in 1912 on Irish mountaineering, in which they reviewed their experience of mountain climbing in all parts of the country, they concluded reluctantly that there was 'nothing to repay a definite climbing visit'[33] to Ireland. There was too much vegetation covering gullies; too many rocks had disintegrated into scree. But the next year, writing alone, O'Brien spoke up for the spirit of adventure that had sent their fathers into the Alps. Ireland, denigrated and dismissed, should instead be regarded as a world ripe for discovery, he argued, particularly the mountains in the west that rise directly out of the sea. '… the geological map', he wrote 'which is striped and spotted, which shows a mountain to have suffered severe crushing and compound fracture … makes one pull the decanter towards one's chair and shout "Eureka." For it is the structure that matters … the hidden forces within the mountain which have determined whether it present the sheer impossibility of the Wetterhorn precipice, the elusive boulder problems of Grey Matilda, or the many-pathed playground of Lliwedd.'[34] 'This is the real joy of the explorer – not to prove the feasibility of a peak of repellent but well-known aspect, but to find a way – in fact the easiest way – through an unknown country.'[35] The results, he

said, may be less satisfactory than conventional climbs but the experience is no less strenuous. He concluded with words that suggested he had had a dispute with Dickinson and was raising a solitary flag for Irish climbing: 'This, the thoughtful reader will guess to be a preliminary to retracting part of my share of the article on Irish Mountaineering in the last Journal. I hope it may be so.'

The following year he persuaded Mallory and Young to attempt Mount Brandon, a craggy mountain that descends steeply into the sea on the north coast of the Dingle Peninsula in County Kerry. Disappointingly the English climbers pronounced the red sandstone unimpressive for climbing and the expedition was a failure. But they were compensated by a week of sailing along the unpredictable Kerry coast with O'Brien's other guests: Dermod, his young son Brendan, and Frank Craig from the United Arts Club.[36]

Climbing with people of such exacting standards in an atmosphere of confident innovation and experimentation was a formative experience for O'Brien and influenced his later yachting career. Small-boat sailing like guideless climbing was relatively new; its parameters needed defining, its possibilities explored. Conor's climbing companions had shown him how a confident, independent spirit could make their enterprises successful and supremely enjoyable. He responded wholeheartedly, both by joining in and by going out on a limb with his individual style and Irish perspective.

Conor and his sister Margaret sailing *Kelpie* on Ireland's west coast c. 1913.

Chapter 3
Sailing

Sounds of water surround the climber: 'the hissing of a streamlet cascading over the cliff, the patter of drops falling from a projecting rock, the rumbling of the river echoing up the valley.'[1] In a boat at sea water has a different sound: 'The ripple of the tide is louder against the vessel's side, and the splash as the lines are cast off marks the beginning of a period of continual sounds of water … from the gentle hissing of foam along the ship's bows … to her part in the full orchestra of the ocean.' These sounds would, in imagination if not in actuality, accompany O'Brien from the moment he first cast off in a west-Kerry rowing boat with a makeshift sail from Derrynane until his last days on Foynes Island.[2]

O'Brien does not record exactly when he began to sail beyond telling us, regretfully, that it was only after becoming an adult. In December 1901 when he was 21 Conor expressed a fear of sea sickness.[3] He probably began in the summer of 1905 or 1906, after he had started working as an architect and was returning more frequently to Ireland, so that his growing prowess as a climber in winter was matched by his growing confidence as a sailor in summer. He learnt slowly, through experience (though he seemed to pick up the rudimentary techniques quickly), valuing trial and error as a method. After a summer sailing in the west-Kerry rowing boat, he hired what he described as a proper sailing boat in Dublin Bay, and, sailing single-handed, discovered that he had not yet adequately mastered the skills of steering and reefing.

His next move was to buy a coastguard whaler for £10, the *Mary Brigid*. She was a sea boat, small and open, that was for a time his 'most cherished possession'. It was by sailing this boat with his two sisters and a local fisherman around the west coast of Ireland, and going from Derrynane to Valentia

to race in the Valentia regatta, that he learnt the small-boat handling that he valued so highly. The west coast of Ireland was a particularly challenging place to learn. Instead of an easy introduction with smooth waters and steady winds there were sudden, all-encompassing gusts, Atlantic swells, successive rocky headlands that protruded far out into the ocean, and off-shore islands, each ringed with its own specific pattern of currents. The rewards were high for, once these conditions were recognised, the sailor could delight in working with forces of an almost unmatched power and complexity.

Conor and his crew sometimes went night fishing with the Kerry seine fishing boat and its follower (both rowing boats). These traditional boats fished with large, fine-meshed nets and the *Mary Brigid* carried fish (often mackerel) if there was a heavy catch.[4] Conor included a description of such a trip in *The Runaways*, evoking the community involvement: the fishermen and then, when they landed the fish, their wives and children, working together. Small-scale fishing had been encouraged in the west of Ireland by the Congested Districts Board in the 1880s, and from 1902 by the Department of Agriculture and Technical Instruction which had introduced co-operative practices. Fish exports grew by about 50 per cent between 1905 and 1910. Conor saw that the short fishing season could be a profitable complement to the rest of the farming year and that small-scale enterprises, which did not involve heavy investment in expensive gear, were ideal. In this he was at odds with the government which, inspired by the increased exports and by the need to promote Irish fishing during the war, would encourage larger scale enterprises with loans for bigger boats that people would find difficult to repay.

Conor was very conscious when he sailed the *Mary Brigid* to Dublin Harbour that she was

Conor's sister Margaret and a friend sailing the yacht *Kelpie* on Ireland's west coast c. 1913.

Kerry fishermen with their seine boats, Derrynane c. 1900.

Photograph taken from the yacht *Kelpie* of the Three Sisters, south of Smerick Harbour, County Kerry, c. 1913.

The yacht *Kelpie* about to anchor off the west coast of Ireland c. 1913.

A Conor O'Brien rigged small sailing boat working the tides off Foynes Island c. 1910.

Kelpie sailing on the west coast of Ireland with crewman, and Foynes islander Jack Finucane on the right c. 1913.

not a yacht and that he and his crew presented an eccentric spectacle to other yachtsmen. In a bold move in 1910 he sold the share in his house in Upper Mount Street and bought a racing man's yacht, *Kelpie*. Over 46 foot long and over 17 tons,[5] *Kelpie*, built in Lymington, Hampshire in 1871, was designed to be handled by a large crew. She was difficult to control, and Conor would afterwards write that he had been an over-ambitious novice to buy her.

He spent the summer of 1910 learning how to sail her with the help of a professional skipper, William Brady. By the end he realised that the boat

was not suitable for Atlantic cruising and a small crew. He began to adapt *Kelpie* to a ketch rig and try out new gadgets. After a few experiments he concluded that the perfect adaptation was elusive, and so emerged the idea that would become an article of faith: that yacht design and boat handling must be guided by experience and responsiveness to circumstances; that there are few definite rules and no perfect yachts. 'When the time comes that I can see nothing about my ship that wants alteration, it will be a token of senility,' he wrote in *From Three Yachts* in 1928. In the summer of 1911 he sailed around Ireland for two exhilarating months.

Chapter 4
Gunrunning

In July 1914 Conor took part in the gunrunning for the Irish Volunteers with Erskine Childers for which Childers is famous and O'Brien hardly known. When Asquith's modest Home Rule Bill proposing a separate Irish parliament with jurisdiction over internal affairs (not including control of revenue, defence, war) had been presented to Parliament in 1912, both the constitutional nationalists under John Redmond and the unionists under Edward Carson assumed it was provisional. Hoping that a larger measure of self-government would follow Redmond accepted the bill; fearing a subsequent larger measure of self-government Carson rejected it. Protestant unionists, particularly those in industrialised Ulster, did not want to be dominated by the poorer Catholics of the south. They were prepared to fight, and the Ulster Volunteer Force was formed in January 1913. The Irish Volunteers were founded in response in November 1913 to defend Home Rule.

In Westminster the Liberal's bill was delayed by a slow passage through the Lords (it no longer had a veto). Under pressure from the unionists Asquith proposed that individual Ulster counties could opt out of Home Rule for up to six years. Predictably, this was accepted by Redmond and rejected by Carson. Outside Parliament the Ulster Unionists upped the ante by running 25,000 German rifles and 3 million rounds of ammunition into Larne, County Antrim, on 24–25 April 1914, an illegal action that the government did not challenge. Arming the Irish Volunteers in the south seemed

a logical step to both radical nationalists and more moderate supporters of Home Rule. Landing the much smaller (and older) arms that they could afford would be a propaganda coup establishing the credentials of the Irish Volunteers. For the radicals any negative government reaction would reveal a unionist bias and the guns could, if a constitutional settlement was not reached, be used. For moderates like Childers and O'Brien a show of strength might pressurise the Liberals to come to a constitutional arrangement.

To maximise publicity 900 Mauser rifles and 29,000 rounds of German ammunition were to be landed in broad daylight at Howth from Erskine Childers' yacht, *Asgard*. A week later 600 rifles and 20,000 rounds of ammunition were landed during the night at Kilcoole, County Wicklow, having been shipped most of the way by O'Brien's *Kelpie*. Although the daylight landing has received far more attention than that at Kilcoole, Conor played a vital role. Conor's independent, sometimes wayward spirit emerges in this well-documented episode in which he was working in close co-ordination with other people.

The initiative for the gunrunning came from a radical. Roger Casement, a member of the Provisional Committee of the Irish Volunteers who had written articles anticipating a war with Germany as Ireland's opportunity, persuaded the London-based nationalist, Alice Stopford Green, to form a committee to raise funds to buy arms. The members of the committee – which included Conor O'Brien, his cousins Hugh O'Brien (he would later become his brother-in-law when he married Margaret in 1915) and Mary Spring Rice, and Erskine Childers – and the gunrunners themselves were Anglo-Irish moderates who did not expect the guns to be used. Despite his nationalist sympathies

Jack Finucane on board the *Kelpie* running before a gentle breeze on the west coast of Ireland, c. 1913.

Conor had joined the navy as a reservist in 1910 and thus also had imperial allegiances. When the Home Rule crisis occurred in 1914 he hoped for a peaceful solution.[1] Erskine Childers had written a well-received book in 1911 arguing for Dominion Home Rule.[2] Gordon Shephard, one of the crew on *Asgard*, was a commissioned army officer who had joined the newly formed Royal Flying Corps in 1912 and used his leave for the *Asgard* trip. Behind the scenes it was Irish Volunteer men such as Bulmer Hobson who were making the arrangements. Hobson was a member of the radical Irish Republican Brotherhood, a fact unknown to most people involved in the gunrunning, including Erskine Childers and O'Brien.[3]

The London gunrunning committee soon raised over £1,500, mostly from its members.[4] As gunrunning was illegal, secrecy was the biggest issue. Mary Spring Rice, an active Gaelic Leaguer, daughter of Lord Monteagle and friend of Erskine Childers, suggested that the guns be brought to Ireland in unobtrusive private yachts.[5] In this she was referring to Childers' best-selling novel of 1903 *The Riddle of the Sands*, in which a small yacht had successfully spied on German naval plans because of its apparent innocence. Childers, ambitious as a military analyst, had written the book as a tract rather than a novel and, at the end of the book, he proposed the creation of a naval reserve composed of small-boat sailors who knew the coast and all its intricacies. Mary Spring Rice was turning this on its head by suggesting that yachts be used against British interest.

She proposed buying and converting an Arklow fishing boat, the *Santa Cruz*, which, as Conor observed 'nothing could make … look like a craft with legitimate business in the North Sea.'[6] Erskine went to Foynes to see the *Santa Cruz* on 21 May 1914 and met Conor who was to re-rig and convert it for the gunrunning. Erskine approved of Conor's ideas but was also doubtful about the boat's credentials. *Kelpie* was suggested as an alternative, but Conor's reputation within his family stood in the way of this. 'M[ary] is dead against Connor [sic] having command,' Childers told his wife, Molly, 'and says he is useless at a crisis and that rules out *Kelpie*

Robert Erskine Childers in Boer War uniform.

which is anyway too small for the purpose, except in the last resort.'[7] Childers proposed his much larger 30-ton *Asgard* instead, while *Kelpie* was brought in for the overflow.

Erskine Childers, Anglo-Irish through his mother and currently living in London, was a slight, unassuming, bespectacled man with a limp. But, ten years older than O'Brien (who was 33), he was a significantly more established figure. He had seen action in the Boer War and written three books on South Africa. *The Riddle of the Sands* had not only made his name but, with its warning that Britain might be unprepared to defend itself against a belligerent imperial Germany, had caught the contemporary imagination. He had been sailing seriously since 1894 – *Riddle* was based on a sailing trip made to the Frisian Islands in 1897 – he had a secure grasp of politics through his (recently abandoned) career as a clerk in the House of Commons, and knew political and intellectual leaders such as Churchill and Bertrand Russell. Added to this he was a man who, once convinced, followed his interest with passion, often to extremes.

Conor's letters to Childers written immediately after the gunrunning indicate that he respected him and would have liked to know him better. Like the mountaineers, Childers had high standards. However, although Childers and O'Brien had much in common, they never became close. The high standards and the elusiveness provoked O'Brien. In the letters, in which he tried to gain Childers' attention, O'Brien gave him a partly confessional, partly self-justifying account of his experience in the gunrunning. He admitted to faults (particularly his indiscretion), which others had complained of and which revealed his own frustrations. Conor also defined himself against Childers. He playfully identified Childers' perfectionism: 'I am sure that you, with your far more obtrusive conscience (that is at least how I diagnose your character) gave yourself an infinity of trouble to keep mathematically in mid-channel!' he wrote, referring to the return journey to Ireland when the boats were filled with guns and the plan had been to stay away from the shore.[8] However, perfectionism, was not, he claimed, something he would always aspire to. He had risked going ashore from the laden *Kelpie*. He continued: 'It is a splendid thing to do everything properly, but if you can't rise to that the next best thing is to do it comfortably.' Conor would strive for the highest standards in his sailing. But he would write about the need for comfort and safety and how, if there was a conflict between practicality and technical prowess, the former should be given priority.

Erskine Childers was more central to the preparations for the gunrunning than O'Brien. O'Brien did not meet Darrell Figgis, the Irish journalist with European connections who was a member of the Volunteers and who bought the guns, in the early stages. (O'Brien first met Figgis when they trans-shipped the guns at the Ruytigen lightship.) However, Childers was with Figgis in Hamburg six days after inspecting the *Santa Cruz* in Foynes, negotiating the purchase of the guns with him. O'Brien was also not told that 'Dolan' referred to Bulmer Hobson.[9]

O'Brien was vaguely aware of secrets kept from him, while his ignorance shielded him from the dangers. Contrary and independent as he could be and temperamentally averse to secrecy, he was outspoken. In his account of the gunrunning in 1963, Bulmer Hobson vented his frustration at O'Brien's indiscretions.[10] He accused O'Brien of being 'talkative to a degree that made him a dangerous colleague for anybody engaged on an enterprise of this sort.' According to him, Childers refused to allow *Kelpie* into Howth because O'Brien would not take reasonable precautions. Hobson argued that their distrust was justified, repeating the story that O'Brien asked two men in Dublin with no connection to the Volunteers (Cruise O'Brien and W. E. G. Lloyd) to advise him about his landing. When the authorities began to search boats around the Irish coast in June, Hobson accused O'Brien of rousing their suspicion with his reckless talk. And he maintained that O'Brien was asked to trans-ship his cargo off the Welsh coast to *Chotah* not because, as O'Brien claimed, *Chotah* had an auxiliary engine and was more likely to make it on time, but because O'Brien had attracted the attention of the authorities.

O'Brien would counter that the risks were taken for practical reasons.[11] In an account written in 1947 he hinted that as they were making preparations he deliberately spread a rumour in Foynes that the *Santa Cruz*, which was being refitted as *Kelpie* sailed out, was to be involved in a gunrunning trip on the principle that truth is less believable than fiction. Further, with people's attention on the *Santa Cruz*, the *Kelpie* could slip out unnoticed.[12] Diarmid Coffey, a young barrister with some yachting experience whom O'Brien knew from the United Arts Club and whom he invited to help crew *Kelpie*, was more sympathetic about O'Brien's outspokenness. 'O'Brien', he said in a radio broadcast in 1961,'believed in talking so much that no one would believe what he said.'[13] Obviously O'Brien did not think that security could be absolute in a small place like Dublin and tried other strategies, however ill advised or unpopular.

Apart from the atmosphere of secrecy the participants in the gunrunning also had to contend with chronic unpredictability. The yachts, all

Mary Spring Rice (right) and Molly Childers with guns and ammunition aboard *Asgard* after 12 July 1914.

George Cahill, crewmember on *Kelpie's* gunrunning voyage.

without engines except *Chotah*, were at the mercy of the tides and winds. They were highly visible, and sailing down the Channel they risked passing the British fleet at Spithead near the Isle of Wight. Who knew what interest they might excite and what delays might occur? Finding crew to sail at unscheduled times to unknown destinations and getting boats ready at short notice was almost impossible. All this could mean that the crucial appointments, which relied on almost perfect timing, might not be kept (the trans-shipment of cargo at the Ruytigen lightship, *Kelpie's* transference of cargo to the *Chotah* off the Welsh coast and the landings on the Irish coast, for example). And there was the risk of a prison sentence and confiscation of their boats if they were caught, something the participants barely mentioned in their correspondence as they concentrated on trying to make the gunrunning a success.

O'Brien, however, did reveal severe doubts about the enterprise, writing to Childers at the last minute to absent himself.[14] It is extremely unlikely to have been a loss of nerve, for O'Brien would prove himself a more than usually brave person on countless occasions. More likely the secrecy alienated him, or he doubted his ability to meet the deadlines in such uncertain circumstances. His last-minute refusal added to the volatility of the situation and worsened his reputation for unreliability. However, he was not immune to the arguments of Mary Spring Rice, and on 29 June 1914 he set out down the Shannon Estuary from Foynes with his sister Kitty as mate and cook, Diarmid Coffey, George Cahill from Foynes and Tom Fitzsimons from Foynes Island.[15]

Conor recorded that his main feeling was the pleasurable sensation of yachting with a purpose.[16] Diarmid Coffey, however, remembered the ferocious conditions and O'Brien's temper:

> It was blowing fairly hard and three of us were struggling with the [top]sail. O Brien had a very hot temper and a fine flow of language but when curses failed he dropped the wheel and brushing us aside did the job single-handed. O Brien had one of the hottest tempers I had ever met and was very highly strung, but under it all he had a very warm and kindly disposition. He would curse one in a ferocious manner one minute and apologise the next.[17]

In five days they were at Cowes on the Isle of Wight where they were to meet *Asgard*. Childers, unknown to them, had had to delay starting so that Conor was forced to wait two days. Nervously aware that their shabby boat and what he described as their rustic crew were conspicuous in highly polished Cowes, O'Brien sent telegrams to Alice Stopford Green to find out what had happened to Childers. When *Asgard* arrived at Cowes both skippers were furious: Childers coldly angry because the telegrams may have drawn attention to them, O'Brien, shouting abuse at Mary (as she had anticipated) because they were late.[18]

Erskine also had a large crew: Molly Childers, Erskine's wife, a lively, intelligent American who had been sailing with Erskine since their marriage, Mary Spring Rice, who was an enthusiastic novice to sailing and did the cooking, Gordon Shephard and two Donegal fishermen. Although it was extremely cramped and the weather had been bad, the atmosphere was very different from the *Kelpie*. Mary, cheerful and capable, performed the domestic chores without complaint and was, Molly told Alice Stopford Green, 'a *great* companion'. Erskine was a sensitive skipper, particularly to his female companions: 'I shall never certainly work for such an appreciative person as you again,' Mary told him afterwards.[19] Shephard, according to Mary's diary, could be lazy and self-centred, but he was also charming and entertaining.

The rendezvous at the lightship was postponed for two days until Sunday 12 July 1914 because of

Foynes Islander, Tom Fitzsimons (on right), crewmember on *Kelpie*'s gunrunning voyage, with Mike O'Shaughnessy, Askeaton, County Limerick.

Asgard's delay. *Kelpie* left Cowes on 10 July in a light wind to travel the 150 nautical miles to the Ruytigen lightship off the Belgian coast. It was calm and hazy as they sailed along the south coast to Dover and then across to Belgium, and they worked hard to take advantage of the tides and rare gusts of wind. By Sunday morning they were in a windless fog, rocked by heavy rollers that were emerging from the mist and disappearing into it again. Ten miles from the lightship, they were drifting slowly in its direction. To prepare for the cargo of guns they ripped out the skylight and hoisted up the gravel ballast, and, as morning turned to afternoon, they

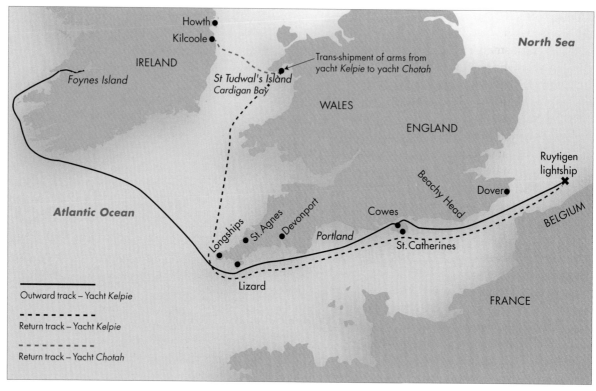

Route taken by *Kelpie* running guns into Ireland, July 1914.

began to look out for Figgis in the German tug, *Gladiator*.

Figgis had been in the vicinity of the lightship since early in the morning, alone in the fog, anxiously aware that he was not quite sure how he would recognise O'Brien.[20] When each appeared to the other out of the mist, suddenly and at close quarters, they had to make a quick decision. 'It just had to be Figgis or we were done: we were already two hours late,' O'Brien later wrote, and he called out to him. 'Luckily,' he wrote, 'it was "in Gaelic".' But Figgis claimed that it was in English and that it was an incriminating '"Is that the boat with the rifles for the Irish Volunteers?" or some words of the like sort'. Both heard with relief the skipper of *Gladiator* asking if Figgis' reply was Mexican. Figgis had posed as a Mexican when he had bought the guns, for the Germans were concerned that the selling of another consignment of arms to the Irish would be used by the British as a pretext for war. It took over two hours to transfer the 600 rifles and

20,000 rounds of ammunition to *Kelpie*, and as they drew away from *Gladiator* at 8 p.m. *Asgard* loomed out of the mist to take her consignment.[21]

O'Brien and his crew set off gingerly in *Kelpie* with their bulky cargo which filled the saloon; from now on they had to recline around a drawing board perched on the rifle bales to eat. They had 12 days to get to the meeting place 25 miles southwest of Bardsley Island on the edge of Cardigan Bay in Wales where they were to meet Sir Thomas Myles. A well-connected Dublin surgeon, a friend of Childers and a Home Ruler, he was the skipper of *Chotah* to which O'Brien and his crew were to trans-ship the guns. The weather was fine for the first few days, but the proximity of the British fleet meant that they could not cruise in comfort, and as they approached Dover they met eight dreadnoughts sailing to Spithead for a review of the entire British fleet on 18 July. The vast steel-grey battleships, alert and heavily armed, formed two lines ahead on either side of *Kelpie* going down the channel. 'I felt I was a very bad kind of conspirator, then I reflected they probably hadn't seen me at all! I was so small,' O'Brien later told Childers, underplaying the tension they had felt.[22]

At the Cornish coast they ran out of bread and, their stove inadequate for baking, they had to risk going ashore at Penzance in their rowing boat, leaving *Kelpie* shrouded in a convenient fog. They finally arrived at the northern end of Cardigan Bay early and again broke the rules, or as Conor put it, 'interpreted the instructions', anchoring and going ashore as a yacht's crew would do, in the belief that it is the ordinary that is inconspicuous.[23] Here there was a moment of tension when their claim to be Breton onion-sellers was met with disbelief by the local publican and pilot. But there were no awkward questions: 'we were merely put down as that unaccountable thing, mad yachtsmen.'[24] When the time arrived to leave the shelter of the bay to meet Myles, it was blowing a gale and the sea was lumpy. They could have waited until conditions were calmer, but Conor decided to stick to their plan. It was, Conor told Erskine, 'a perfectly gratuitous piece of punctiliousness (but I am a very punctilious person)'. After a night being blown about in the gale, *Kelpie* returned to St Tudwal's Island where they found the sensible Myles safely anchored. When it got dark they warped alongside *Chotah* and trans-shipped the guns along with most of the crew except Kitty, another manoeuvre that was criticised for being risky because it was in view of the coast.

The plan had been for *Chotah* to motor across the Irish Sea the next day to land the guns in Kilcoole on Saturday 25 July. This would distract the coastguard's attention south before the Howth landing at noon the next day. But *Chotah*'s mast had split so the Kilcoole landing was postponed for a week. O'Brien, probably acting on his own initiative, substituted *Kelpie* as decoy. He set sail for Dun Laoghaire on the morning of the Sunday when *Asgard* was due to land the guns. He anchored off Bray, aware that his yacht looked travel worn and empty while he, visible on the hatch, cleaned a rifle. A destroyer and the coastguards ignored him but he was able to tell a credulous reporter that he had just landed guns in Wexford.[25] Meanwhile *Asgard* had

arrived at Howth and at midday met the Volunteers at the pier. They unloaded the guns, watched at a distance by a coastguard cutter. *Asgard* slipped away before the naval patrol could arrive and the Volunteers marched into Dublin. There was a tragic coda to this for, baited by onlookers in Bachelors Walk for their inability to capture the Volunteers, an army detachment fired on the unarmed crowd, killing three people.

A week later on the evening of Saturday 1 August Kitty and Conor took the *Mary Brigid* to Kilcoole where they joined the other small boats receiving guns from *Chotah* anchored at Ballygannon Point. They landed them on the beach by the lights of the railway station.[26]

There is no doubt when all the published accounts and O'Brien's unpublished letters to Childers are put together that O'Brien acted responsibly and that his contribution was valued. Bulmer Hobson devoted a significant section of the chapter on the gunrunning in his 1963 book on the Volunteers to O'Brien's failings, but his concluding sentence exonerated him: 'Although I make this criticism of Conor O Brien he was a wonderful seaman, a charming person, and he rendered us very great service.'[27]

The conflicts with O'Brien largely arose because O'Brien differed from Childers and Hobson in the methods of maintaining secrecy. O'Brien was highly attuned to the workings of communities. He was alert to the impression that different types of boats and their crews made on each other, each with prescribed roles and expected behaviour. It was a drama with which O'Brien himself was never entirely comfortable (he often felt that, as the skipper of a relatively modest-sized yacht, he was underestimated) and as a result he observed it keenly. Many of the risks he took during the gunrunning, making contact with other people, arose from his belief that *Kelpie* and her crew would not be the object of suspicion if people were able to pigeonhole them as yachtsmen on an early summer cruise and so dismiss them. He aimed at invisibility rather than subterfuge.

There is an element of playfulness in this calculated courting of danger and it is clear that

O'Brien enjoyed himself. 'I envied you awfully for the run to Howth, but we had quite good fun last night,' he wrote to Childers the day after they landed the guns at Kilcoole. He was still getting fun out of it years later when the guns could be associated with armed rebellion. In his novel *Two Boys Go Sailing* the boys discuss the owner of a boat, *Kelpie*, with a retired colonel.

> 'What? What?' barked the Colonel. 'Do you really *know* that swab?'
> 'Why – er – yes, in a way,' the Mole stammered, quite unconscious of what he'd put his foot into.
> 'Don't you know what he did with her in the end?'
> The Mole could say with truth that he didn't.
> 'He was gunrunning, sir. Running guns for the rebels – for that murderer Collins. He ran her ashore on the Scottish coast to avoid capture. He saved his dirty hide and left the poor ship a total wreck.'[28]

O'Brien felt that the gunrunning finally made a sailor of him. 'I am awfully glad I went on this trip,' he told Childers, confidentially. 'I had always before been a horrid coward on the water, especially in the way of imagining shipwreck when I ought to have been asleep. This month at sea has given me absolute confidence both in my ship & in myself, and I really learnt a whole lot of seamanship into the bargain.' Then, with the self-deprecation that was characteristic of this period, he added that he and Kitty came to grief soon after trying to sail the much smaller, unballasted *Mary Brigid* to Kilcoole. 'It really was a comedy – as we had thought ourselves really expert small-boat sailors at the least'.

The gunrunning assignment with its emphasis on the self-reliance and skill of the individual suited O'Brien, as it suited Childers. It must have confirmed O'Brien in his growing conviction that small-boat sailing was a challenge he wanted to explore.

Childers had given a powerful expression of the qualities needed for this life in his portrayal of Davies in *The Riddle of the Sands* based, several biographers have convincingly argued, on himself.

O'Brien too possessed many of these qualities. Davies, the owner of the diminutive and spartan *Dulcibella*, is self-sufficient, resourceful and modest. 'You're so casual and quiet in the extraordinary things you do,' observes Carruthers, the self-confident Foreign Office man who is accustomed to conventional sailing with large crews. O'Brien too was capable of passing off the remarkable as ordinary but he did not have Davies' patience. However O'Brien would inadvertently cultivate many of Davies' attitudes. He knew how to make cramped quarters homely and when to pull out the champagne. He too would adopt a sea-centred view of the world, regarding the shore as an inferior element, a source of necessary supplies. He would be technically adept and inventive, but not impose his knowledge boorishly. And he would appreciate the innate subversiveness of small-boat sailing in which an individual is allowed to pit himself against the elements and, inevitably, find himself critical of a too-ready acquiesence to the idea that conventional society was civilised.

The gunrunning was linked to the political fortunes of Home Rule, and it coincided with the events leading to the outbreak of the First World War. On 21 July, while *Kelpie* was sailing towards Wales and *Asgard* was anchored at Milford Haven, Asquith, having abandoned the Amending Bill that was to deal separately with Ulster, called a conference in which the nationalists and unionists were to decide on a solution to Home Rule. This collapsed on 24 July. When the guns were landed two days later and with the subsequent tragedy of Bachelors Walk, the impossibility of a constitutional settlement seemed to be underlined.

When he returned to Dublin after trans-shipping the guns to *Chotah*, Conor felt that Ireland stood at the brink of catastrophe, a feeling perhaps partly aroused by a sense of guilt for his part in running the guns. On 31 July he wrote to Childers, 'I feel this afternoon as if I were living on a volcano. This country is trembling with military evolutions, & I am awfully afraid of the extremists taking charge & making the gravest trouble. Noone seems to be quite sure what the Volunteers' position is.' Like John Redmond, Conor underestimated unionist opposition to Home Rule. He naively imagined that the Volunteers could nominate a provisional council chosen from all parties that would be pledged to colonial self-government and which could come to an agreement with the Ulster Volunteers to frame a constitution for Ireland. This would, he hoped, proclaim its power, something that would be acceptable to an England which 'I am sure [would] do anything in reason to get shot of the whole country', and then send a deputation to England 'to guarantee the peace and integrity of Ireland'. If England did not acquiesce he thought Ireland would be in a position to carry on government without her consent. He did not imagine that this would mean an Anglo-Irish war. These were ideas, he told Childers, that were frequently aired in Dublin. Unrealistic as they were, they point to the panic generated by the breakdown in talks.

On 28 July 1914 Austria declared war on Serbia. By 31 July the British First Fleet, fresh from its review at Spithead, was at its war station in Scapa Flow. On 4 August, three days after the Kilcoole landing, Britain was at war with Germany.

For Asquith and the Liberals the war immediately superseded Ireland as the issue *du jour*, and on 18 September Home Rule was placed on the statute book to be put into operation with special provision for Ulster when the war was over. For nationalists too the war came as a relief. John Redmond, anxious to force through the Home Rule Bill and a Home Ruler who saw no paradox in supporting the war, pledged Ireland's support in an emotional Commons speech on 3 August. As Britain had entered the war in support of neutral Belgium the principle was established that they were fighting for the rights of small nations: something that appealed to nationalists. He thus urged the Volunteers to join the army. Most did, though a significant proportion did not. Conor, taking up his naval duties, could fight for Britain with a clear conscience.

Chapter 5
War Service

When war was declared Britain, with its superior navy, was able to establish a blockade of Germany, by closing off southern and northern exits to the Atlantic with the Channel Fleet stationed at Portsmouth, and the First, later Grand, Fleet at Scapa Flow in the Orkney Islands. Thus Germany was largely cut off from supplies of food and raw materials from beyond Europe. The east coast of Britain was defended with patrol flotillas, and naval ports were defended with local defence flotillas.

Instead of trying to engage the British fleet in a decisive battle that they would almost surely have lost, German strategy was to pick off individual ships within patrols using mines and U-boats (submarines) armed with torpedoes. This aimed to lessen the numerical superiority of the British fleet and to destroy merchant ships with their precious cargoes. As both U-boats and mines were difficult to discover and destroy, the Germans posed a significant threat to British shipping. For much of the war the British tried to counter this hidden threat by sweeping mines and hunting submarines. For this they needed small, armed boats, many of which would be manned by volunteer reservists. It was only a qualified success.[1] Towards the end of the war the Admiralty accepted that convoys were the best way to reduce the menace of submarines.

Conor O'Brien's war experience was directly related to the defence of British shipping from mines and submarines and to the change in Admiralty attitudes: for most of the war he was employed on small, armed boats; towards the end he was accompanying convoys to the Mediterranean in naval ships. The war was a turning point for O'Brien

Conor O'Brien in Royal Naval Reserve uniform
c. 1915.

as a sailor for, after a number of mistakes, he became exceptionally experienced in handling boats and crew in many different circumstances, and he learnt how to channel his independent-mindedness. Without his war experiences it is unlikely that he would have contemplated, let alone carried out, his circumnavigation.

Conor had been a member of the Royal Naval Reserve (RNR) – the body set up in 1859 to train professional seamen for the navy – for at least four years before the war and had had a Merchant Navy training. In February 1910 he had taken a gunnery course in the Royal Naval barracks in Devonport.[2] Despite his prior commitment it was not until the end of January 1915, six months after the outbreak of the war, that O'Brien took a course in minesweeping on HMS *Defiance*.[3] He was a temporary sub lieutenant. On 2 March 1915 he was appointed to command a fishing trawler, HMS *Lord de Ramsey*. It had been converted to a minesweeper and was operating out of Newhaven.[4] It was common practice to convert fishing trawlers with a sweeping wire and to man them with fishermen and RNR or Royal Naval Volunteer Reserve (RNVR) officers. That O'Brien felt overwhelmed by his new responsibility is suggested by one of the few comments he made on his war experiences in his books. In *From Three Yachts* he described wanting to make contact with Jack Gardner of Brixham after the war, 'the man who had saved me from utter despair when I was pitch-forked into the command of a steam-trawler manned otherwise on deck (for I had a treasure in my engineer) by the most amazing collection of incompetents it was ever my misfortune to sail with.'

On 9 April the *Lord de Ramsey* grounded because O'Brien miscalculated the tide. Men could be court-martialled for this but O'Brien was merely cautioned to be more careful in future.[5] Soon after this he was discharged for misconduct, and his association with the RNR ceased. He spent the New Year holiday on Lliwedd with Mallory and other climbers.

O'Brien did not let his mistakes in the RNR spell the end of his war service. On 4 April 1916 he joined the RNVR, the civilian naval reserve for non-professional seamen. He was again given the rank of temporary sub lieutenant and, as his records put it, allowed 'a fresh chance', though frequent reports were to be made on him.

On 15 April he was sent to HMS *Hermione* (known light-heartedly as 'Hermy-one'), an old (1893) cruiser moored at the motorboat patrol depot in Southampton, for a course of instruction. At some point he did a gunnery course at the Royal Naval barracks, Portsmouth. In a surviving censored letter to Dermod informing him that he was about to go on the course, Conor asked him to send clothes for Reserve men: sweaters, sea-boat stockings, gloves, mufflers and caps. 'At least', he added, 'that's what I want – bar the first of which I have four!' He ended the letter: 'I'm afraid I can't tell you what my job is till the war is over. It is not confidential – its secret. So you can imagine anything you like, always remembering that I am a cautious & gunshy person.' This was secrecy with which he was comfortable, although even here he could not resist throwing out hints.

He was appointed as a gunner on a motor fishing boat, *Twilight*, from 20 June to 1 September 1916. Life on board *Twilight* was monotonous. She was part of a flotilla patrolling the fishing nets on the short stretch of water on the Firth of Forth between Granton in Edinburgh and Inchkeith, an island in the Firth used as a naval base. Occasionally *Twilight* went to Kinghorn on the north coast. The weather was bad – they were often in mists and fogs – and the log is devoid of events, except the single occasion when they examined the fishing permits of two fishing boats outside the half-mile limit.[6] However, the lack of excitement no doubt meant that they were successful in keeping submarines submerged and unable to fire torpedoes.

On 1 September 1916 O'Brien was sent on another *Hermione* course on navigation, ship-

Conor O'Brien with his sister Margaret, both in Royal Naval Reserve uniform c. 1915.

handling and the duties of a naval officer. This course was designed to train RNVR temporary officers to command motor launches which had arrived from Canada in early 1916 to augment the fleet of small, mobile, patrol craft used for hunting submarines around the British coast. They had diesel engines, carried a gun, and employed a naval crew. On 16 November 1916 O'Brien was given command of one of these motor launches for four months. The temporary RNVR officers were not highly trained (though O'Brien was more highly trained than most) and learnt by their mistakes as they weathered storms and an enemy that was professional and experienced. In the absence of Royal Navy personnel and in the unprecedented circumstances on these small boats, rules and discipline were rudimentary and improvised, a challenge one can imagine O'Brien enjoying. As with his experience on *Twilight*, the success of this posting was largely measured in the uncountable submarines that remained submerged. It was a life that encouraged a dependence on seamanship, the use of technical knowledge, ability to cope with mental and physical strain and an understanding of the value of discipline, all qualities that O'Brien would need to sail around the world and which he would celebrate time and again in his subsequent books.

On 22 March 1917 he was given a command on HM Yacht *Sayonara*, a large, motor-driven vessel that had been requisitioned for the war to patrol harbours and carry light stores to major ships. Just under two weeks later he was promoted to temporary lieutenant.[7] He stayed on *Sayonara* for 26 months until 25 July 1918 when the ship was decommissioned. O'Brien was getting an intimate knowledge of the British coast and at least part of his time on *Sayonara* was spent off the west coast of Scotland. She is reported to have been off Mull in October 1917, and O'Brien recorded that the yacht often put in at the Scottish island of Rum for fresh vegetables. On one occasion they stayed longer so that the captain could stalk deer, and Conor took the opportunity to climb the mountains.

Just before he left *Sayonara* O'Brien was examined in seamanship and navigation and gained a second-class certificate. Two months later he joined the gunboat HMS *Kildare* as a navigator. *Kildare* was a new ship, built in April 1918, and was used to protect convoys travelling to the Mediterranean. The Admiralty had been very slow in appreciating that large convoys protected by armed escorts and travelling in a zigzag course were the answer to the U-boat threat. Convoys were as hard to locate as single ships, difficult to attack and able to counter-attack immediately. U-boats were a particular menace in the Mediterranean because of the number of choke points through which traffic had to pass, and in 1916 nearly half the ships sunk by U-boats were lost in the Mediterranean. The convoy system had finally been introduced in May 1917 and 'through convoys', running from Britain to Port Said, first ran in October 1917. By the time Lieutenant O'Brien joined *Kildare* on 27 October 1918 such runs, known as Danger Zone Escorts, were well-established fortnightly events and appreciated as a successful strategy.[8] Like patrolling, success was measured by the absence of excitement. 'Convoy work was boring and unglamorous. Some escorts spent months, or indeed the whole war, at sea and never saw, let alone, engaged, a U-boat. The most successful convoys were those on whose voyages nothing happened.'[9]

Kildare set sail from Milford Haven a week after O'Brien's arrival on board. The size of the convoy is not recorded in the log, but the daily uneventful zigzagging down the Atlantic is. The convoy anchored at Gibraltar for 24 hours to acquire stores, and it arrived at Port Said on 18 November. By then the armistice with Germany had been signed. However, convoy work did not immediately cease, and *Kildare* set out for Milford Haven on 1 December with five ships. O'Brien stayed with this ship for a year; he was demobilised on 14 March 1919. He had proved himself to be an officer with good command qualities. The navy had kept him at sea, reappointing him to different ships when many were sidelined into staff jobs ashore.

Several of the men involved in the 1914 gun-running fought bravely in the First World War. Gordon Shephard had been immediately mobilised as a flight commander in the Royal Flying Corps when war was declared, and by February 1917 was a brigadier general. He was awarded the military cross, the Distinguished Service Cross (DSC) and the rank of Chevalier of the *Légion d'honneur*. He was killed in January 1918, making a routine flying tour of the squadrons he commanded. Erskine Childers joined the Royal Naval Air Service (an arm of the RNVR). He instructed pilots in navigation on the HMS *Engadine*, served in the North Sea and in the eastern Mediterranean, and, ignoring regulations, flew himself on several occasions. He was also decorated with the DSC. Sir Thomas Myles served with the Royal Army Medical Corps, becoming a lieutenant general. Although unsympathetic to the 1916 Rising, he remained loyal to Volunteers who had unloaded guns with him at Kilcoole. One of these was Eamon Martin. When Martin was wounded in the Rising of 1916, Myles, working at the Richmond Hospital, found him a bed there and when Martin became the subject of police surveillance, engineered his escape by disguising him in his British officer's uniform.[10]

O'Brien's skill and commitment to sailing was recognised after the war in September 1919 when he was elected to the Royal Cruising Club (RCC). This club was founded in 1880 to facilitate small-boat sailors in the pooling of information and experiences, and by 1919 had a distinguished membership. O'Brien was proposed by an early member, Frank Gilliland, and seconded by Erskine Childers.[11]

Chapter 6
Fisheries Inspector

Conor's base in Ireland shifted during the war. Since selling his share in the Upper Mount Street house he stayed in 76 Waterloo Road and 44 St Stephen's Green when he was in Dublin to see Dermod, use the IAOS offices on Merrion Square and meet his friends at the United Arts Club.[1] But the appeal of the city had diminished; Dickinson now worked in England and the pre-war conviviality and high spirits had largely evaporated. Increasingly he went to Foynes Island.

This small, broad-backed, rocky island, separated from the mainland by a narrow sound, provides the shelter that makes Foynes so favourable as a port. It is itself a microcosm of the mainland with the same shaly shore, a mirroring network of fields, the familiar sequence of inlets and promontories, open hillside and concealed paths, salmon weirs, landing places, traces of the iron age, and a Napoleonic gun emplacement. It has a self-sufficiency, a containable smallness and completeness that makes it like a child's idea of an island. And, with the provisions and conviviality of Foynes in close proximity, life on Foynes Island was at once both less definitively isolated and more self-consciously separated than life on the many islands that shadow Ireland's coast and dot its rivers.

Like many of these islands, Foynes was inhabited in the early twentieth century. There were six families living there, but most of the land was owned by a branch of Conor's family.[2] In 1915 Hugh Vere O'Brien, an engineer and an officer in the Royal Munster Fusiliers, married his second cousin, Conor's sister Margaret, and was given a large portion of Foynes Island as a wedding

Aran Island fishermen – photograph taken by Conor O'Brien during a west of Ireland cruise on the yacht *Kelpie* c. 1913.

present. After the marriage the couple moved to Monare, a comfortable nineteenth-century house set among mature trees overlooking the sound on the sheltered southeast of the island.

At first Conor went to the island for Margaret's sake, for Hugh was away fighting. Hugh emerged with the Military Cross and wounds which affected his mobility for life. Hugh and Margaret's children were born after the war: Elinor in 1918, Murrogh in December 1919, and Turlough in 1923, although he, sadly, died ten years later. The family stayed on the island, the children enjoying the freedom before they were sent away to school. They had close ties with several of the local families, particularly Michael and John Finucane. These brothers, who farmed and fished and worked in the orchard beside Monare,[3] lived with their parents and two sisters at the back of the island.

In the early years Conor used the island as a base for his County Limerick architectural work, and for sailing to the west coast. In this it replaced Derrynane, and from now on Conor's sailing interludes would start and end on the estuary's wide water, running with the tide past the gently rising land punctuated here and there by a tower, fort, castle, village or big house. Gradually, Foynes Island took hold of his imagination, and he would return frequently to the only place that he felt to be his home.

Post-war and then post-independence Ireland was a difficult place for Conor to settle into. At first he had his architectural work. This had continued on and off during the war. He had designed a simple hall for the Kilmallock Co-operative Friendly Society in October 1914, and a memorial in St Mary's Cathedral for Dean Lucius O'Brien who had died in 1913.[4] For the latter he had proposed a cut-stone surround, decorated with a series of squares based on King Turlough's tomb in Ennis, for

Detail of the lettering designed by Conor and cut in 1921 for the war memorial in St Mary's Cathedral to his brother Aubrey O'Brien, killed on 1 November 1914.

Detail of carving designed by Conor from the reredos in St Mary's Cathedral, 1907.

the north door in the chancel, and a simple, precise inscription. The final text, decided by Dermod, was inscribed on two, unsatisfactory, thin brass plaques fixed to the stone.[5]

After the war there were the sad demands for memorials. Saddest of all was the memorial for his younger brother Aubrey, killed in action on 1 November 1914 at the First Battle of Ypres. This had been a fierce battle of hard shelling and two German attacks. Aubrey, a lover of parties, cricket, horse-riding and Cahirmoyle had got a commission in June 1902 when he was 20. By 1914 he was a captain in the Royal Field Artillery.[6] Conor produced a handsome cut-stone panel which was placed next to Lucius's memorial and shared its square motifs. This time the inscription in simple raised Arts and Crafts-influenced bronze lettering was an integral part of the design.[7]

Conor liaised harmoniously with Dermod and the vestry over Aubrey's monument (it was started in about 1920, the inscription was cut after April 1921 and it was finally erected in 1923) but he had more trouble with a war memorial that the cathedral commissioned. This was proposed in March 1920 and was under the control of his uncle Donough and the vestry. 'Here is your beastly war memorial,' he wrote to Donough in January 1921.

Although Conor's suggestion that the memorial be in stone had been accepted, the men's names were to be in cost-cutting brass and now extra names had been added so that the design had to be simplified. But Conor's main frustration arose from a difference of opinion about whether to record the men's regiment (the usual gesture) or where they lived. Conor's arguments reveal that despite his five years' experience fighting in the navy he was sensitive to the view of the war held by those in Ireland without strong ideological beliefs, who had lost sons, brothers and husbands. He was also aware of the political status of the war in Ireland in January 1921.

It seems to me that it would be much more distinctive to put the people's place of origin rather than their regiments on record. There might have been half a dozen Pat Connellys in the Munsters, for instance; and if they only joined up for the war their relatives probably wd not have any particular sentiment about the regiment, but would like to have them identified as the people of this county who are the ones who would see the memorial. However I am aware that those things are not dictated by logic & commonsense, so if you tell me to put in the

*regts I will do so, & if you insist that I must be
snobbish & give their rank, I will do even that.
But to my mind one does not want, especially at
the present time, to commemorate the Army, but
certain of our neighbours who have died.*

Regiment and rank trumped place. The memorial,
a slightly odd stone structure just inside the door
of the cathedral, is decorated with a carved stone
floriate plaque and an inscription in more of the
simple raised lettering – this time in polished
limestone – that is O'Brien's distinctive contribution
to the cathedral.

Work on the memorials proceeded in tandem
with a commission to reorganise the layout of the
cathedral and design a chancel screen, which he
did in partnership with Richard Orpen, an architect
in Dublin since 1888 who had worked on several
Irish cathedrals.[8] This kept Conor intermittently
busy throughout 1921. The screen, finally erected
in December 1922, is cleverly based on the panel
tracery of perpendicular gothic windows. It has a
straight top with a frieze beautifully carved with
foliate shapes that are variations of those found on
the reredos. At the base of the screen is an Arts and
Crafts bronze grille and gates; together they frame
the reredos and Dermod's mosaic triptych. The
architects' fees and expenses came to £221 7s 9d.

O'Brien did not particularly relish this long
drawn-out work for the cathedral. On 12 April 1921
he wrote to Dermod; 'I shall be tied by the leg to
the cathedral for the next three months, I suppose.'
Although busy with current projects he seemed
to have no new architectural work. His focus was
shifting from architectural commissions for the
IAOS and the Church of Ireland as he tried, using
the skills as a sailor honed during the war, to find
a different role in the newly evolving Ireland.

Nationalist expectations in Ireland had changed
radically during the war. The Rising in 1916 had put
violent revolution and republican ambitions back
on the agenda, and the execution of the leaders had
given Sinn Féin unprecedented popularity, even
though the party had not been directly involved
in the Rising. In the election of 1918 Sinn Féin
won 73 out of 105 seats. The Irish Convention of

1917–18, in which the British had attempted to
settle the pre-war issues between the unionists and
nationalists, had failed. In January 1919 the elected
Sinn Féin representatives refused to take their seats
in Westminster, setting up their own assembly and
alternative government, the First Dáil, in Dublin in
January 1919. It was proscribed by the British that
September.

Many who had supported Dominion Home
Rule before the war were dismayed by the Rising
in 1916. Erskine Childers, later a fervid republican,
was particularly disgusted with Roger Casement's
role in looking for German assistance for Irish
nationalists during the war when they were
Britain's enemy. However, Conor, at the house of
nationalist sympathisers in Dublin at the end of May
1916, vocal in his disbelief of rumours that someone
else had been posing as Casement, expressed some
knowledge of Casement which suggests that he
had some sympathy for him and possibly for the
rebellion.[9]

When Conor returned to Ireland after the war
it was clear to him that Ireland's future lay with
Sinn Féin, a party that was attracting both radical
and more moderate nationalists. Dermod, on the
other hand, now supported the constitutionalist
Nationalist Party. Both made their politics known,
Dermod even proposing to stand as a parliamentary
candidate in west Limerick in 1918, although his
offer was rejected by the party leader, John Dillon.
But this political difference does not seem to have
come between the brothers.

Conor had definite ideas about how the self-
proclaimed Irish government should deal with
the fisheries, and he approached the Dáil with a
co-operative scheme of joint purchase and sale
for organised fishermen in order to keep their
expenses down and improve their marketing.[10]
This was in tune with the thinking of the First Dáil,
which, drawing on long-term Sinn Féin policy, was
keen to promote co-operation. Dáil members had
also identified the underfunded and disorganised
Irish fishing industry as an area which, with some
informed policy and not too much capital, could
show quick improvement and win the government
points in the propaganda war with Britain. On 28

November 1919 the cabinet created a Department of Fisheries and appointed Sean Etchingham as director.[11] His policy was to stimulate the industry with loans to newly established co-operative societies to buy vessels and equipment. Eight co-operatives were established within a few months, of which five – in Baltimore, Dingle, Ring, Gorumna (Connemara, County Galway) and Tory Island (County Donegal) – received loans of nearly £20,000 from the National Land Bank.

It was, unfortunately, a disaster. At least two boats sank, money disappeared, and there was deep distrust between the Dáil cabinet and the fishermen, the fishermen accusing the politicians of incompetence who accused the fishermen of dishonesty. In March 1921 the cabinet stopped the loans. Given the circumstances, failure had the edge on success, for the new government was, almost from its inception, acting against a background of war. The Anglo-Irish War had its beginnings in January 1919 with the murder of two Irish policemen by the Irish Volunteers (soon known as the Irish Republican Army) and escalated with the deployment from August 1920 of regular British troops, including the soon notorious Black and Tans. The fighting involved attacks and reprisals of terrible ferocity, often in rural communities. The terror, destruction and chronic uncertainty affected everything the fledgling co-operatives depended on: communications, morale, markets.

The government, which had had no time to form an effective administration to give it a secure formal presence in the fishing communities, relied on reputation and experts. Conor would have come to their attention through the IAOS and through two of his former gunrunning companions who were already employed by the government: Darrell Figgis, who had been appointed secretary of the Commission to Investigate the Resources and Industries of Ireland in June 1919; and Erskine Childers, who had been appointed a director of the Land Bank in April 1919. (The bank was set up by the government to lend money for the purchase of untenanted land but was also used for projects like the fisheries programme.) Conor, delighting in the idea of political friction, speculated that he was

employed to silence his criticisms of Dáil policies; more realistically he knew he was one of the few who was prepared to work at sea, an advantage when ambushes and attacks made road and rail transport perilous and unreliable.[12]

Conor's first mission was to investigate a controversy in the Dingle co-operative in the spring of 1920 with Childers and Eoin MacNeill.[13] Their recommendation that the loan be increased to £40,000 was met with dismay by the Dáil, which voted only £1,630 for Dingle in March.

Far more stimulating was Conor's solo summer assignment to act as a fisheries inspector to the new co-operatives; he was charged with finding out how the loans were being spent and to warn societies that were mismanaging their finances. (A Dáil committee was appointed to investigate the societies on 6 August 1920.[14] In his account of this period in *From Three Yachts*, Conor gave several explanations: he claimed that Michael Collins, the Minister for Finance, had written off the loans as a bad debt, and was using Conor as a way of establishing the presence of the republican government in remote fishing communities; he also described himself as an inspector of fisheries, investigating loans; finally, he said he was winding up co-operatives, although it is unlikely that he had the authority to do that.) His field of operation was the entire west coast of Ireland: from Baltimore in Cork in the south to Tory Island off the Donegal coast in the far northwest. It included the coastal waters and the fishing communities – what he lucidly described as 'the unco-ordinated units of co-operation' – scattered about the heavily indented coastline and off-shore islands. He sailed with his sister (probably Kitty) as mate, a female English journalist with an articulate and provocative response to the seascape, and two fishermen who acted as crew.

A yacht on the business of an illegal government, they sailed a fine line. To appease the British coastguards, Conor refused to engage in any smuggling, however innocuous-seeming, and replied to any signalling with Naval smartness. 'It is a great mistake to jeopardise by petty smuggling a reputation which may be wanted any day to bring off a large coup,' O'Brien wrote later with boys' own relish.[15] To reassure the fishermen he kept *Kelpie* unpainted and utilitarian. The coastguards were seduced by the glamour of the yacht, despite its lack of black and gold paint, and he was never searched for guns, state documents or cabinet ministers. And the fisherman, he felt, gave him all the help he needed.

It was a good summer for Conor. He enjoyed the frisson of danger: 'it was rather risky to be too well received by either party for fear one might be shot by the other'. He fell more deeply in love with the west coast. Not only did the clear, deep waters and well-defined hills lessen the hazards for Conor and his crew, but he discovered the great multiplicity of sheltered places secreted about the promontories, islands and tortuous indentations of the coast and the people who lived about them. He returned to these days many years later when he wrote *The Runaways*, a story about boys sailing the west coast in a stolen boat, drawn unresistingly into the world of men on the run.

Conor was still in *Kelpie* in December. But by then his spirits were low. He had found too much incompetence, both in Dublin (the societies had not been organised on proper lines) and among the enthusiastic but uninformed volunteers, who had no chance against powerful vested interests.[16] And he had been drawn into the marginally illegal local schemes which he disliked. On 9 December, while he was waiting for *Kelpie* to be repaired in Baltimore, he told Dermod that he had recently set out for Milford to sell fish but instead he had had to 'dispose of' contraband butter. 'However, I hope to forget all about fish very shortly,' he continued. 'As soon as the Kelpie is finished I am going to Foynes, & someone else can take on this job which at present consists of writing letters to Smith Gordon & waiting for replies which never come.'

But Conor's frustration did not disappear on his return. He spent much of the early spring of 1921 working on the re-planning of St Mary's Cathedral with a reluctant vestry, and becoming increasingly disillusioned with co-operation. In March 1921 he wrote to Dermod complaining that the co-operative societies did less business than they should because they failed to encourage members to deal with them, did not look for new members, had insufficient capital and were uncompetitive. 'I am rather disgusted with things. The whole movement is living on charity – or at least on the bank guarantees of a few philanthropists – & it ought to be self-supporting by now.'[17] Dermod shared his frustrations: 'Worry, worry, worry. Poultry and eggs a rotten failure treated co-operatively. Philanthropy, the worst of vices and crimes . . . I.A.O.S., D.A.T.I., C.D.B. etc., etc., more than half philanthropy, a bad thing as it all tends to keep Irishmen from standing on their legs and facing their difficulties with their fists up.'[18]

Dermod was an important influence on Conor. By the early 1920s he was a successful painter of society portraits and landscapes in Ireland. He made a good living, mainly from the portraits, had been president of the Royal Hibernian Academy since 1910 and had refused a knighthood. He was a strong character and had a subtle influence on many people. Lennox Robinson, who knew him well, evoked some of this when he described Dermod's periodic visits to his wife and family at Cahirmoyle: 'On his arrival everything in the house unconsciously pulled itself together. One sat straighter in one's chair, the parlour-maid waited a little more swiftly at dinner, even the fire in the library seemed to burn more brightly, the logs behaved themselves.' Dermod was relieved when he was finally able to sell Cahirmoyle to the Oblate Fathers in 1920 and buy the spacious 65 Fitzwilliam Square in Dublin. Writing to his son Brendan before the sale Dermod revealed how much he had disliked the responsibility of the estate: 'I am glad that you take the proposed move from Cahirmoyle philosophically … its an awful millstone about one's neck to feel compelled to go to a place that is away from the interests of your life.' The future, he added, was uncertain for landed proprietors; the position occupied 50 years previously in his father's time had gone for good.[19]

Conor and Dermod remained close. Conor still to some degree relied on Dermod's strength of character and his support. He was someone to whom he could express his feelings and political beliefs even when he knew Dermod did not share them. So when Conor was in Limerick city on the occasion when the police reacted brutally to a bomb and gun attack by beating unarmed women and men it was to Dermod that Conor wrote of his frustration and sense of powerlessness. 'What can an unarmed citizen do?' he asked rhetorically. He had reported events he had witnessed to the army, but, he added laconically, 'I don't suppose anything will come of it, unless it be a bullet in my back.'[20] He accused the authorities of inciting the gunmen as 'an excuse for further outrages', 'which', he added, 'makes one think they did away with O'Callaghan and Clancy [mayors] because they discouraged reprisals.'

He also confided his doubts about his future to Dermod. His plans were dependent on the uncertain circumstances in the months before the truce: 'If the south are making another push at coop fisheries, which I hope they will, & if they want me back again, which is unlikely, I shall of course have to go. If there is still no govt I shall go somewhere peaceful to recoup my nerves, & I think Margaret will be about ready for the same treatment. Meanwhile I'll think about the P.F.'

The best way for Conor to regain peace of mind was to embark on a challenging sailing expedition, which is what he did in the summer of 1921 after the truce on 11 July, which ended the Anglo-Irish War. It culminated in disaster.

The challenge was to sail *Kelpie* single-handed from Dun Laoghaire to Foynes around the north coast of Ireland, with a detour up the west coast of Scotland. Conor was not too worried about co-ordinating the various sailing tasks on his own, but he did fear that *Kelpie* could not be trusted to steer herself while he cooked, ate or slept. But after his first night's sleep in which the boat moved steadily in the right direction, he began to think of the ship as his companion and felt closer to her than ever. After a few days he met a friend, Matthew Botterill, in *Molly* and persuaded him to anchor and do some climbing on the Scottish island of Rum. This was followed by a storm in which *Kelpie* dragged her anchor, her gear became unrove and O'Brien had to

spend the night on *Molly*. O'Brien's fears that *Kelpie* had sunk were unfounded and he left for Oban the next day. The following evening he retired to the saloon, lit a pipe and wrote up his journal, confident that although he was in a relatively narrow channel full of other sailing vessels *Kelpie* would not hit anything. Later he was woken by the jolt of an impact. 'I knew at once that it was all over; I had killed my poor little ship. She, who worked for me unaided night and day, found me asleep upon my watch, and for all her virtues the reward was her destruction.'[21]

He had not only lost a boat but he had lost the nearest thing to a home: 'Her end came so quickly that I hardly realised my loss till I stepped ashore on the quays of Portpatrick in the grey light of dawn, to find myself homeless, earth-bound, and dependent on others for my movement.'

After the truce came the Treaty of December 1921 and the establishment of the Free State. By June 1922 the country had slipped into civil war. Conor offered his services to the Free State, courting an Irish general in Tralee: 'I heard he had been agitating for an armed trawler & I wanted to get command of her if he was successful. I am afraid however there's not much chance of getting her. We haven't as a nation any enterprise at all about maritime affairs.'[22] There was more demand for his literary skills: W. G. Fitzgerald asked Dermod if Conor would contribute a chapter on the mercantile marine in his compendious survey of Ireland, *The Voice of Ireland*. Pessimistic about the fisheries Conor was scathing about the marine, but offered to write on church architecture.[23]

During the uncertain time between the Treaty and the Civil War O'Brien had embarked on a new enterprise. *Saoirse* had been designed and built in the first six months of 1922. This success suggested a new career. 'I am taking up boat building', he told Dermod in December 1922. He had another definite and one possible order. However, six months later he would be leaving Ireland in *Saoirse* to sail around the world. A very different career was in the making.

SAOIRSE

Yachting World, December 1957. The cover features a photograph of *Saoirse*, when owned by Erick Ruck, sailing off the southwest coast of England.

Chapter 7
Saoirse

In 1922 O'Brien was 42. Sailing and climbing in bare feet had made him physically fit and extremely agile. A photograph taken a few years later in 1926 standing between two men from Cape Clear Island, Denis and Con Cadogan (who would crew the *Ilen* to the Falkland Islands) reveals the attractive physicality of O'Brien's presence and his innate confidence. He stands upright and faces the camera squarely, his hands behind his back. He is wearing creased knee-length shorts, the pockets bulging with tools, and a white T-shirt, which reveals the strong muscles of his upper arms. It is several days since he has shaved and his hair is unbrushed. His casual appearance, his ease and something in the directness of his expression are modern. Next to him the Cadogans – with their worried expressions, uncertain postures and more formal clothes – can be more precisely placed as working men from the early part of the twentieth century. It is only when O'Brien's confidence is interpreted as reflecting his social position – Ascendancy captain and owner of the boat – that he recedes slightly, though not much, into the past.

O'Brien enjoyed feeling the sun and the wind on his body. When he got to sea he stripped and felt that once he was burnt he had acquired a protective layer. Several photographs exist of O'Brien on his yachts bare-chested or in a vest, and in all he appears contented and at ease. He might be taking the sun in the tropics, pulling at a rope, or looking at the sky: every time he seems to be in his element. In contrast he looks slightly awkward and self-conscious when he is photographed wearing a jacket, even in the shot on board *Kelpie* in which he is also wearing shorts and has bare feet. In one photograph published in his account of the circumnavigation, *Across Three Oceans*, in which he is shown at the helm dressed in captain's uniform – blazer, cap, bow tie – a cigarette in his right hand, with Kioa, the man who sailed with him to Ireland from Tonga, standing behind him, he seems to be posing for the camera. There was in fact an element of presentation in this even though his clothes were authentic, for this is what he wore when he approached a port.

Other people have commented on O'Brien's physical presence. His nephew, Murrogh, Margaret's son, who grew up on Foynes Island and was a boy when Conor visited in the 1920s and 1930s, remembers his short, steady walk, often in bare feet, the quick way he could scale a tree and his ability to cut off branches while precariously balanced. Maurice Griffiths, who sailed with O'Brien in the 1927 Fastnet race, described Conor's compact physicality and energy, and hinted at an inherent mischievousness which he associated with O'Brien's Irish background; '[O'Brien was] short, stocky, red-haired and with merry blue eyes and a tanned elfin face, was full of fire and Irish jocularity'.[1] In his autobiography, Conor Cruise O'Brien recounts the often-told story of O'Brien whipping a journalist from the unionist *Morning Post* on the steps of the Kildare Street Club: 'I suspect there was a personal as well as political source for the ferocity of Conor's resentment,' he wrote. 'Conor had deep-set eyes, extremely thin lips and a barrel chest. I have never seen a human being who looked more like a gorilla.'[2] Where Murrogh admired his uncle, Conor Cruise had less goodwill for his godfather.

Conor approached the design of *Saoirse* with carefully formulated ideas. His aim was to design a boat for ocean sailing that would be capable of about 150 nautical miles a day if the crew worked hard, that was forgiving, safe in all weathers, and that had a steady motion. He also wanted a level of interior comfort that would make living aboard desirable.

Interior of *Saoirse* by Kitty Clausen, 1931, pastel, published in *Voyage and Discovery*, 1933.

Saoirse running before a light breeze in the Mediterranean, c. 1934.

Because of financial constraints it had to be a small boat – 20 tons and 40 foot long maximum (though the boatbuilders would add two feet in the attempt to save the boat from complete inelegance, or, as O'Brien put it 'for the sake of their reputation').[3] A small boat would enable him to employ a small crew or, if necessary, to sail the boat single-handed. He wanted as much speed and comfort that would be compatible with a short waterline length and relatively heavy displacement. In balancing these things he had set himself a classic design challenge such as his mountaineering companion, the architect and industrial designer David Pye, and the Arts and Crafts designers of his English and Dublin circles would have relished. Like these designers O'Brien embraced constraints, regarding them as moral guardians: 'Only the man who is forced to be content with the minimum, who has to do most of his own work, gets – I will not say what he wants, but what is good for him.'[4] Working

within such focused constraints also encouraged economic design solutions and a tendency towards simplicity for both practical and aesthetic reasons.

The saloon was comfortable – large, high with a generous rooflight (high and long) and, with relatively few cupboards, spacious. It had a swinging table to accommodate the ship's motion.[5] This level of comfort was achieved at the expense of speed, for the saloon's size was maximised by putting the mainmast further forward than was normal. O'Brien's great innovation was to take the stove out of the forecastle where cooking was a hazardous business in high seas, and put it in a galley at the rear of the saloon where the ship's motion was gentlest and the act of cooking more pleasurable. O'Brien frequently commented on the need for a good cook, especially on long voyages, and he appreciated cooking as 'a delicate and important operation'. He was keen that the galley be conducive to culinary innovation in the best

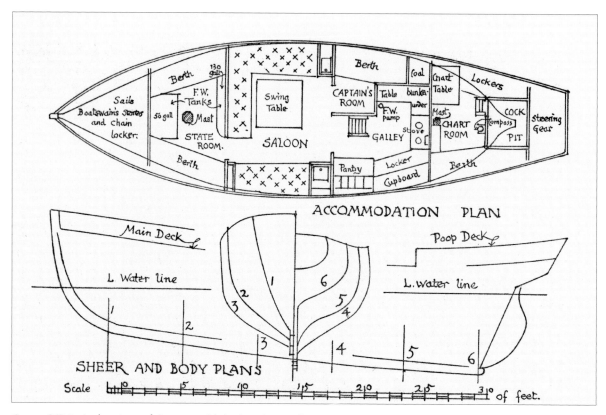

Conor O'Brien's drawings of *Saoirse* published in *Across Three Oceans.*

conditions and to simple delivery in the worst. The centrally placed stove was also important for heating the ship. This repositioning of the galley not only made a long cruise more viable but would encourage O'Brien to use the ship as a home.

Saoirse had a raised poop deck, an old-fashioned feature at the time, which made for greater buoyancy and thus comfort in the oceans where the wind often blew from behind. O'Brien decorated it with turned balusters which, sturdy and simple in themselves, gave the ship a slightly antique character.

O'Brien designed the deckhouse with a view to self-sufficiency and practicality. He equipped it with a bunk and chart table close to the helm so the helmsman could call his replacement without waking other crew. There was also a window in the forward bulkhead so that the helmsman could keep an eye on the stove. These small but significant details made a great difference to working

conditions: 'I attribute a great deal of Saoirse's success to [the deckhouse]', O'Brien wrote.

O'Brien gave *Saoirse* a ketch rig. The relatively small sails of a ketch rig were easier for a small crew to handle, which was what O'Brien had in mind for sailing the yacht, and might even be managed by himself, alone. It was also economic, for O'Brien was able to cannibalise *Kelpie's* sails, a significant saving when new sails might come to 40 per cent of the total cost of a new boat. He adapted the rig during his circumnavigation when the wind was behind him by using a square sail. The ship was lit by acetylene gas and there was no engine.

Sitting in Monare on Foynes island with an improvised drawing board, looking across the sound to the sawmill and timber yard in the village, O'Brien fantasised about getting his ship built there, despite the lack of a boatbuilding tradition, and thus stimulating an industry. The more realistic option,

Tom Moynihan, Fishery School Master Shipwright of *Ilen* and *Saoirse*, standing at the quay in Baltimore c. 1968.

however, was to have the ship built at Baltimore.

Baltimore, a small town on the heavily indented coast of west Cork, commanded a substantial harbour dotted with islands and ruins. Poverty stricken since at the least the mid-eighteenth century, it had failed to capitalise on the fish in its local waters. In 1887 the parish priest, Fr Charles Davis, and an English philanthropist, Baroness Angela Burdett-Coutts, had set up an industrial fishery school specifically to stimulate the local fishing industry. The boatbuilding element had been given a commercial dimension by 1898. In 1904 a new slipway and a stone, boatbuilding shed were constructed, both of which still exist (the latter, unfortunately, in poor condition), and by 1912 the shipyard had a good reputation. This was largely due to Tom Moynihan. He had been a pupil at the school and was now the shipwright in

charge of the yard, designing and superintending the construction of coasters, trawlers and yachts and repairing naval and private craft. He worked with O'Brien on the design of *Saoirse*. He could also supply well-seasoned oak, able tradesmen and a competitive price.

There was much about the boatbuilding process that excited O'Brien:

> I think a boat looks best when the frame has been set up and the planking just begun. You can see all the graceful curves of her timbers, each differing slightly from its neighbours, but so closely related to them as to carry the eye easily over the intervening space, so distinct as to give a sense of form and perspective hidden by the smooth skin of the finished hull ... Certainly *Saoirse*

Saoirse sailing along the south coast of England when owned by Eric Ruck, c. 1965.

Saoirse ghosting along parallel to the coast in the late 1920s. O'Brien, experimenting as ever for coastal voyaging, has converted *Saoirse* to a staysail schooner.

looked best at this stage, for she is stout, not to say tubby, rather than elegant, and seems extravagantly large when the whole of her body is exposed. Now, however, she looked impossibly small to contain all the luxurious cabins I had planned to fit into her: as I stood on her midship floor-timber the deck-beam was little above my head, and the space seemed to taper away to nothing with extraordinary rapidity towards her ends.[6]

He rejoiced in the use of grown timber: the curved pieces of oak used for the frame came from the branches of trees and had to be seen and chosen before they were cut; a 'trade of the hand and eye'. O'Brien was fascinated by the mysterious shaping and fitting of straight pitch pine planks to form

a smooth curve. And he revelled in the building shed: the activity focused on the gradually emerging ship, the pungent small of freshly cut wood. He later included a description of boatbuilding in his novel *Two Boys Go Sailing* and commissioned his niece, Brigid Ganly, Dermod's daughter, to draw the boatshed for the frontispiece so that it is a leitmotiv for the book. Boatbuilding was a contemporary window onto the medieval past for O'Brien, evoking the workshops and yards out of which the great Gothic cathedrals had risen. It was the Arts and Crafts designers' vision applied – not in a landlocked rural setting in which wheelwrights, furniture makers and stonemasons were the heroes as it was in southern England – but to a shipyard in a remote corner of County Cork where the shipwright ruled.

Illustration of a boatyard scene from *Two Boys Go Sailing* by Brigid Ganly.

However, O'Brien's moments of euphoria were interspersed with long periods of intense frustration. In the tense period between the Anglo-Irish War and the Civil War when *Saoirse* was built, west Cork was dominated by republicans who had rejected the Treaty of 1921. Building supplies and men were difficult to get – it seemed to the impatient O'Brien that the ship would never be completed – and there was distrust between O'Brien and the shipwrights. This tension was fuelled by O'Brien's high standards and constant interventions, but it was rooted in politics and came to a head at the launch. O'Brien, the Free Stater, worried that the republicans would hijack a yacht with such military potential while the republicans were suspicious that O'Brien was preparing for the defence of the Free State. There was an argument over which flag should be raised as *Saoirse* slipped into the sea. O'Brien drank all the champagne, 'because I wanted it most after the anxieties of getting the vessel launched and … of getting her away', he later wrote with a lingering note of petulance.[7]

Basing *Saoirse* on a traditional model used by fishermen rather than on the newer racing boats, O'Brien demonstrated his lack of concern for current yachting convention. However, he was not alone in this. Members of the Royal Cruising Club, the yacht clubs of Ireland and the new breed of professional boatbuilders such as Colin Archer who had designed *Asgard*, were also adapting traditional designs for small yachts. Many of these were smaller than *Saoirse*, such as the 11-ton yawls designed by Mulne and built on Belfast Lough before the First World War. *Saoirse* was later acclaimed for the ingenuity of the interior arrangements and for what would become an innovative rig. It has been described as a golden period of boat design. The innovations had a direct impact on sailing, inspiring the owners of small yachts to plan longer and more adventurous cruises.

O'Brien's ambition for the yacht and his possible role in her was expressed in the name *Saoirse*, Irish for freedom. He gave varying explanations for this choice: 'I named my boat in part to commemorate [the] establishment [of the Free State of Ireland]', he wrote in *From Three Yachts* on page 94. Thirteen pages later he described looking at the recently finished *Saoirse* in Baltimore, overwhelmed by her size and his ignorance of how she would behave in the water and he realised that his ambition to sail *Saoirse* single-handed had been unrealistic: 'I thought what a fool I was to suppose that my boat really meant, as her name did, Freedom, and that I could go where I chose in her without help or hindrance from the rest of the world.' The name embodied O'Brien's current preoccupations and hopes: independence for Ireland, independence for himself, and somehow, perhaps, the association of the two.

Conor spent the summer and autumn of 1922

sailing around the west coast of Ireland; there were pleasure trips with his sister Kitty and cruises transporting people and mail cut off by the civil war fighting. Inevitably they were involved in a number of incidents, which – judging by the dry tone in which O'Brien described them – he enjoyed, at least in retrospect. The most dramatic and ironic was being taken for a republican in Valentia: '... appearances were against us; we had been in Bandon last night, and that was a Republican stronghold; we came in a yacht, and it was well known that all hostile acts were performed by or with the aid of yachts; there were two Englishmen in the yacht, and Childers, who was an English yachtsman, had recently cut the cables here (Valentia lives on its Cable Companies).'[8] The army was informed and an officer boarded *Saoirse* late at night accusing them of conspiracy with republicans. He was rude, emphasising his points by banging the muzzle of his revolver on the cabin table. O'Brien may have come under suspicion because his fellow gunrunner, Erskine Childers, was now well known as a propagandist for the republicans. He would be shot by the Free State on 24 November 1922.

Chapter 8
Around the World

O'Brien was reticent about what motivated him to sail around the world, adopting the self-deprecating explanation that his circumnavigation was a piece of serendipity, the result of missing a climbing appointment in New Zealand. Although in retrospect this seems to be an effort to downplay his achievement, it is likely that O'Brien set out with the notion of a circumnavigation at the back rather than at the forefront of his mind. Sailing was such a profoundly unpredictable endeavour that it is unlikely O'Brien formulated a single ambition to be pursued unreservedly, as sailors with more advanced technology have done subsequently. Instead he sailed in stages, from one place to the next, dealing with the winds and waves, keeping a close eye on the behaviour of his boat, for, having designed a yacht that was beginning to approach his ideal, the next step was to sail her and see how she performed.

The self-deprecation was no affectation. O'Brien belonged to a class and an era where challenges were personal tests that allowed one to think well of oneself, rather than an effort to gain a public reputation. Sailing around the world resembled the mountaineering challenges of the Climbers' Club, and paralleled George Mallory's post-war ambition to climb Everest. O'Brien, Mallory and their contemporaries were being faithful to the optimistic pre-war spirit that valued human courage, skill and ingenuity; they were cultivating the vision of individuals successfully pitching themselves against the elements. However, there

Crewman on *Saoirse* on the final leg of O'Brien's great voyage.

was another strand to O'Brien's adventure. The war had given O'Brien a rigorous professional training and prolonged experience of the challenges of sailing at sea. And in the post-war world many activities that had been sport or leisure activities before the war became full-time endeavours and a way of life. It was a period of spectacular physical feats and the inauguration of world records, where, eventually, reputation would become important.[1] Although Conor was not interested in establishing an impressive reputation, the nurturing and development of technique and craft was deeply attractive to him; he embarked on his sailing exploits as an amateur, but he advocated and developed a professional attitude and knowledge in his subsequent writing.

Circumnavigation in a small boat was a preoccupation of the early twentieth century. The American, Joshua Slocum, had established a standard when – the first to do so – he sailed around the world single-handed in 1895–8 and published a book on the voyage, *Sailing Alone Around the World*, in 1900. This inspired several others, so that George Muhlhauser was returning from his circumnavigation in the *Amaryllis* as O'Brien set out in *Saoirse*. Slocum had sailed to Tierra del Fuego and through the archipelago, but few of those who had followed him had descended far into the southern hemisphere – they used the Panama Canal and sailed in a westerly direction at higher latitudes. None had rounded Cape Horn.

O'Brien had a vivid engagement with the history of sailing. He cherished a memory of seeing the *Oweenee*, a large commercial sailing ship, leave Dublin for Newcastle in 1913. He was an avid reader of logs and sailors' accounts, scouring second-hand shops for out-of-print books. As he read he conceived the idea of sailing the clipper route. The clippers were multi-masted, nineteenth-century sailing ships that had carried gold, wool, grain and manufactured goods to Australia and China and returned with tea. *Cutty Sark* was the most famous. They took an easterly route. Leaving Britain they sailed down the Atlantic to the Roaring Forties in the southern hemisphere to sail east, with the Westerlies behind them, across the Indian and Pacific Oceans. They rounded Cape Horn and returned across the Atlantic.

One great challenge of the clipper route was to sail in the Southern Ocean where the Westerlies blow unimpeded around the world so that the waves accumulate to mountainous heights. The other was to round Cape Horn with its threat of ice and rugged waters. This was a region that was dangerous enough for experienced professional sailors in relatively large ships. For the amateur skipper with a small 42-foot boat and a crew of two or three, reliant only on sail and without any means of communication, it was daring, even heroic. When he returned to Ireland two years later O'Brien's achievement was significant: he had been the first to make a circumnavigation in a small boat rounding all three capes – the Cape of Good Hope, Cape Horn and Cape Leeuwin (south-western Australia) – as the clippers had done. Other small boats would follow O'Brien, and by the 1960s it was being done solo: Francis Chichester sailed in *Gipsy Moth IV* around the great capes in 1967; and Robin Knox-Johnston in *Suhaili* and other competitors in the first Golden Globe round-the-world, non-stop race sailed the same route in 1969.

Sailing across the oceans was a venture which was at odds with much that O'Brien had been doing until 1923: it would take him away from his family and social network, from architecture, from his existing sources of income, from Ireland. This may have been its attraction, for it allowed him to circumvent the difficult question of what role he could play in independent Ireland. At the time it may have seemed to be a temporary solution, but when he returned to Ireland he embarked on a previously uncontemplated writing career.

One of the most time-consuming and difficult aspects of the preparations was finding crew. The chances of discovering two men who understood the demands of keeping a small yacht sailing for extended periods, had experience of deep-water sailing and would, within the command structure of a boat, also be companions for O'Brien were very small in Ireland in 1923 (or indeed elsewhere). O'Brien, who, contrary to tradition, had placed his sleeping quarters amidships, in order to be with the crew, would be shocked when, during the first part of his voyage, his mate told him that two people living and working in close proximity should have cabins at either end of the ship and never speak.[2] However, when he subsequently engaged two very able but taciturn men as crew, he was inclined to regard this idea more favourably, although he could never quite rid himself of the desire for a companion, which for O'Brien meant a social equal with similar tastes and experiences.

Concerned to find men who had experience as deckhands (rather than the more passive experience of those who sailed in large yachts with big crews), O'Brien engaged two men who had sailed in boats smaller than *Saoirse*. Sidney Lavelle was the able seaman who also acted as cook and steward, and H. S. Hodge, the mate and a certified chief officer.[3] Used to the danger of falling overboard, they were at first too tentative. And Lavelle may not have been as experienced as he claimed, for seven days into the voyage he was concussed by the mizzen sheet in a relatively gentle force 3 wind.[4] But he was an enterprising man who had got himself a commission to write about the voyage for *The Irish Times*. His reports, written in the upbeat tone of popular journalism with their unabashed expression of current prejudices, reveal a less thoughtful, less literary and more conventional man than O'Brien; someone whom O'Brien might well, in different circumstances, have avoided. *The Irish Times* took a photograph of the three of them just before they departed. Lavelle is a dashing figure dressed in a yachting jumper. He looks straight into the camera with a smile on his young, handsome face, while O'Brien, in a suit and tie, smiles more stiffly. Hodge, also young and informally dressed, looks directly at the camera. But as with the Cadogans, O'Brien is effortlessly in charge, the two men flanking him in

Saoirse departing Dun Laoghire Harbour on the first leg of the around-the-world voyage, 1923.

the photograph, supporting themselves on various parts of the ship, are working harder to make an impression.

The financing of the voyage was another anxiety. Money was needed to pay the crew, equip the ship and obtain supplies and – an incalculable expense – pay for repairs to *Saoirse* during the voyage. O'Brien needed a guarantee to enable him to draw money in foreign banks. Dermod was Conor's staunch supporter in this. He wrote a letter of guarantee for Conor and provided the finance with Lionel Smith-Gordon, a businessman committed to co-operation who had worked for the IAOS, been appointed managing director of the Land Bank in April 1920 by the First Dáil, written extensively on co-operation in Europe and Ireland and was a close friend of Dermod's.[5] Conor achieved publicity and income by writing a series of reports for *The Irish Times* on the voyage, which he sent back at intervals.

Saoirse was not insured. This meant extra pressure to make sure that the voyage was a success and that the ship came back intact.

Although O'Brien was setting off in the wake of historic ships he was very conscious of the benefits available to him in 1923: tinned food, accurate charts of winds and currents. But compared to the equipment of a modern voyage, his was primitive. He had no radio or electronic devices; only a barometer, thermometer, sextant and two chronometers, one set at Greenwich Mean Time, the other for local time. He had no faith in the former chronometer – although the constancy of such instruments had improved in recent years – and checked it at several locations on the first half of the voyage. He also carried a camera.

Apart from assembling charts and buying equipment, a process which he relished and would highlight in adventure stories such as

The Runaways, O'Brien also familiarised himself with ship's business: the bureaucracy associated with the control of goods and disease when a ship enters and leaves foreign ports. Leaving Ireland he had to obtain a Clearance Label, which he would use at foreign ports to prove that *Saoirse* carried no cargo, and a Bill of Health, needed before the crew could land in a foreign port. Despite the Bill of Health – a clean one was signalled by hoisting a yellow flag on arrival in port – they would all be subject to quarantine and could not disembark before they had been inspected by a designated doctor. After that the maritime authorities would ask for a list of passengers. O'Brien made sure that the crew were on articles of agreement.[6] There may have been a financial incentive not to do this but O'Brien felt that the yacht would get through port business more easily if its crew were all officially working and there were no passengers.

Preparation for the voyage was a process of accumulating responsibility for O'Brien. First the ship and then the men: the first was by now a familiar responsibility, the second relatively new. In the 1920s the master had the authority to punish members of the crew who transgressed the articles, and in the ports he was personally responsible for their behaviour. O'Brien did not feel that the rise in status consequent on his assumption of responsibility was recognised in Ireland, for *Saoirse* was too small to merit much respect. He trusted it would be different in foreign ports.

O'Brien set off with the perhaps naïve hope of circumnavigating the world in a year but, as the ship's articles put it, with the expectation of sailing 'to any part of the world, terminating … within two years'. Three stages were planned: first it was south, down the Atlantic to Cape Town; secondly, around the Cape of Good Hope and east across the Indian Ocean to Tasmania; and thirdly, across the Pacific, around Cape Horn and north, up the Atlantic, back to Ireland, the longest and most gruelling leg. He needed to do the journey as quickly as possible because he had limited finance and because, once at sea, they could only carry a certain weight of stores. There was also the constant threat of boredom on long hauls.

There were in the event many more stops en route than he anticipated and he was delayed several times. He was tempted to turn back from Africa and he tried hard to sell *Saoirse* in New Zealand. He was only 280 days at sea out of a total of 730. But they were 280 days amid what he saw as the ever-varying topography of ocean waves: scaling 'long round-backed hills', fighting their way through 'ranges of snow-capped peaks', 'dancing along ridges and furrows rippled before the mild Trade Wind'. There were the gales, dolphins, flying fish and whales, lost land birds and albatrosses, the stark presence of subtropical islands. There was beauty and adventure in the danger, which he never regretted. O'Brien summed this up with practised understatement: 'On the whole it was worth while',

Saoirse was ready by mid-June. To the trained eye she was an odd sight outside the Royal Irish Yacht Club in Dun Laoghaire Harbour: a ketch-rigged yacht with a working-boat air that set her apart from the more status-conscious vessels around her. She flew both the Irish tricolour and ensign of the Royal Irish Yacht Club (to which O'Brien belonged) with the union canton (Union Jack). In foreign ports the latter would be more important, for in 1923 the tricolour was not universally recognised. In fact one of O'Brien's objectives was to proclaim the new Irish state and he flew the tricolour with missionary zeal.[7]

After their send-off from Dun Laoghaire they found themselves basking in the warmth of the Portuguese Trades far sooner than they expected. O'Brien stripped off and enjoyed the sun, but could not relax. He anxiously consulted the barometer and thermometer, and found it hard to leave either crew alone on watch. But there were no mishaps. In fact the conditions were near perfect. 'The good north-east wind held steady, freshening day by day; the blues seas rolled up astern, each day steeper and with a heavier crest of white; the foam lapped over in the waist and hissed along the rail to the bows; and our wake showed green further and further astern.'[8] After twelve days they anchored off Funchal in Madeira and stayed four days. It was O'Brien's first foreign port. Equipped

Saoirse running before the Portugese trades with O'Brien at the helm, 1923.

with ideas about the niceties required to make a good impression he used them successfully: he found an agent to make his purchases; he flew the national flag on arrival and let off a few rockets on departure. They set sail on 6 July and sailed south to the Canary Islands. They observed the steamers plying between the islands – they encountered far less shipping than O'Brien had anticipated – and after the Canaries they lost the Trades. O'Brien was enchanted by the effects of *Saoirse*'s cabin lights shining through the rooflight in the early dusks: 'The brilliant jet of acetylene in the saloon threw the shadows of the rods of the skylight all over the gleaming sails like the ribs of a huge fan which was white to port, where the light fell on the foresail, and

reddish to starboard over the tanned mainsail.'[9]

They anchored in Porto Grande in St Vincent in the Cape Verde Islands, 385 miles west of Senegal on 15 July. Here O'Brien reset his chronometer. He had discovered that Hodge could be slow to take on tasks, and he often made mistakes. It occurred to O'Brien that he might replace him and he made preliminary enquiries. He was taken aback by the response: there were no available sailors. He prepared his rig for the doldrums and South-East Trades by stowing the foresail and its gear. After three days they sailed on towards the southwest.

This first part of the journey was like passing through a series of portals which took them further and further away from home. Yet oddly they did not seem to be passing from the familiar into the completely unfamiliar: O'Brien waited for the moment when they would finally pass into what would seem to be another world. After the Cape Verde Islands they entered a torpid zone of smooth seas, mildew in the stores and flying fish, which even the rigorous O'Brien endowed with fabulous qualities. O'Brien was temperamentally resistant to sailors' yarns and only too aware that he would be expected to supply tales of the extraordinary. Yet several times on his circumnavigation he would be amazed by what he saw, and playfully asserted at the beginning of his account of the voyage, 'I would not ask the scientist to believe the things I have observed myself or have heard from credible people.'[10] 'The truth', he wrote, 'unless decently veiled in myth and romance, is too startling for credence.' About the flying fish he observed, 'I am prepared to swear that they can and do fly … at least … by vibrating their wings.'

They waited anxiously for the doldrums, expecting calms alternating with squalls, torrential rain and lightning. In fact they had sufficient wind and only encountered sperm whales and pilot fish, nothing freakish. They crossed the equator on a smooth sea. Once in the southern hemisphere there were adjustments to be made: the sun in the north at noon, and a new and wonderful panorama of constellations.

They now entered a period in which O'Brien and the crew would be alone together for nearly

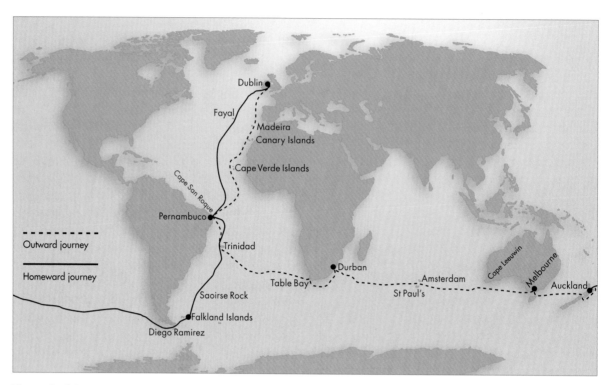

The track of *Saoirse*'s pioneering circumnavigation in 1923–25.

four weeks. O'Brien would never write fully about his relationship with the men while they were sailing, even in his fairly frank letters to Dermod. But in his later accounts he hinted at the tensions between them. Of the sixteen men who sailed with him over the whole voyage O'Brien found that only two were enthusiastic and entirely reliable. The others made mistakes or were inept: there was 'the man who was supposed to be a certified officer and could not splice a three-strand rope … the man who could not go on deck even in the Tropics without putting on rubber thigh-boots … the man who jammed the windlass, and let go the anchor by lifting the pawl and tried to check the chain by dropping it in again'.[11] These were intensely annoying, but their generally poor standard at helm could, in some circumstances, be dangerous, and O'Brien had to keep vigilant. At the time he was frequently impatient, in retrospect he often felt he was to blame. But he was also almost impossible to satisfy:

The things that jar on one's nerves after three weeks at sea, or on any long and rather monotonous journey, are inconceivably trivial, but nearly all travellers know and fear them. If your mate has not exactly the same tastes and habits as yourself, you are irritated because everything he does is wrong; if he has the same the case is worse, because you are annoyed at his lack of initiative and do not give him credit for doing anything at all to help the ship along. My pet vice is an affectation of economy, both in labour and material; and the other fellow always seems to be doing things in the most wasteful way. If he practised economy in his own way I should call him mean; if he tried to find out my wishes I should curse him for asking silly questions.[12]

O'Brien was an exacting skipper. But this was perhaps unavoidable, given his mission; 'The business of the seaman is to accomplish his voyage in safety, first of all, but then as quickly as is reasonably compatible with comfort.' Safety, speed and comfort were all concepts about which he, and arguably any skipper, had strong opinions, and his definitions and priorities held sway. This was acceptable, for the men expected to take on Captain O'Brien's standards. Less tolerable was O'Brien's propensity to find fault whatever the crew did, and Lavelle and Hodge did not buckle down under O'Brien's unpredictable rule. They resented O'Brien's irritation – Conor described them as 'touchy'; his mate had 'more charm than discretion'.[13] They could, it seems, be as temperamental and outspoken as O'Brien.

However, Lavelle made sure that they ate well, particularly in calm stretches when he had time to prepare Irish stews, cottage pies and curries, or when they caught fish, such as the large bonita Conor landed one morning at 6 a.m. Lavelle also tried to dissipate the tensions by suggesting debates at dinner, 'which, curiously enough, caught on, and we now each choose a subject in turn and take the chair. On the whole, they go down well, seldom getting too warm', he told his *Irish Times* readers.

They ate formally on 5 August, traditionally observed as the height of the sailing season, for, as O'Brien observed, 'Yachting is yachting on the 5th of August, whether in Cowes or one degree south of the line.' The next day O'Brien noticed that the masthead had shifted. They hove to so as to give the boat an easier motion, to straighten the mast. They also scraped her bottom which, not lined with copper, was prone to collecting barnacles. This slowed the ship down and was one of O'Brien's constant concerns. They took photographs: one taken from the rigging and published in *Across Three Oceans* shows O'Brien at the helm with the vast ocean heaving behind him, a reminder of how isolated they were. That night there was a sudden squall and the spar finally split. It would need to be repaired as soon as possible. They would not make Cape Town to the east but would have to go 700 miles west to Pernambuco (Recife) in Brazil, for repairs.

They arrived on 12 August and stayed for three weeks, their first delay. Pernambuco welcomed them with a blaze of light. O'Brien delighted in the white palaces that lined the shore and the domes and towers that denoted the older quarters. He immediately felt it was one of the most beautiful cities in the world. But he failed, much to his disappointment, to respond emotionally to his first sight of the New World on the far side of the Atlantic. He was always uncomfortably aware that he could not rise to emotional expectations, happier to make discoveries by accident. He was surprised and gratified by his reception. He was a person of consequence, invited to the consulate, to the captains' room at the ship-chandler's, a captain on a bona fide foreign voyage who got his stores duty free: 'It seemed the most natural thing to be travelling about the world in command of a vessel.' It was a confirmation of the seriousness of what at times he had feared was an anomalous endeavour.

He was made to feel the weight of his responsibilities, for the crew ran wild. Lavelle in particular lived extravagantly, running up debts which O'Brien had to pay.[14] O'Brien was incensed. He would have loved to sack them, but, as he told Dermod, he did not yet have the courage, and he left Pernambuco with them, resigned to their behaviour as a necessary evil. He gave a light-hearted gloss to this episode in his article for *The Irish Times* on 1 November 1923: 'In several moments of irritation I invited my crew, singularly and individually, to desert; but they did not do so; they know a comfortable ship when they see it.' Lavelle gave his version in his *Irish Times* report: 'At last we have got clear of Pernambuco where, although we had a really topping time, we found life very strenuous, with the result that we were out of form and were prostrate for two days.' This report also reveals the arrogance and ignorance that O'Brien had to deal with: 'The natives, pleasant, humorous and healthy, are very nearly white, or appear so, and are busy workers. The majority of the women, in my opinion, are very good-looking, intelligent, and, in some cases I have seen, with perfectly clean-cut features.'[15]

O'Brien's project to be an ambassador for the newly created Irish state was doomed to frustration: 'We have made a valiant attempt to show the Irish flag in Pernambuco. It was not

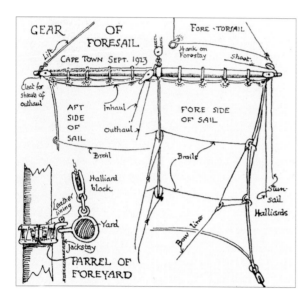

Conor O'Brien's rig detail drawings, published in *Across Three Oceans.*

our fault that the local Press persisted to the last in describing us as English naval officers and locating Dublin in England', he told *Irish Times* readers.[16] He adopted a worldly persona, revelling in the irony. He was not above a literary allusion – 'Nothing in Pernambuco became us so well as our leaving of it', he began, paraphrasing a line from *Macbeth*[17] – and he embroidered freely on their encounters with the pre-disembarkation bureaucracy, suggesting that they only got out through the use of subterfuge and guile. However, the vivid picture of O'Brien setting off a departing rocket with a lighted cigar has an authentic note.

Leaving Pernambuco they passed through another portal and embarked on the 1,250-mile stretch to the island of Trinidad, a run he had nervously earmarked as particularly difficult when he had first planned the voyage. In fact they had an easy passage, fanned by a light breeze over smooth seas. Then, an hour before sunset a black peak broke out of the canopy of cloud to announce Trinidad. The place beguiled O'Brien. Unlike the Caribbean island of the same name which can, he wrote with a touch of disparagement, be visited by mail steamer, this Trinidad is remote and deserted. 'There is to me a singular romance about these tiny

outposts of earth pushed a thousand miles into the waters; barren masses of volcanic rock, once milestones on the course of clipper ships threshing to the southward for their long run to China or Australia, but now rarely seen by human eye.'[18] He revelled in the fact that it had been named by a passing explorer and was almost entirely unknown to his contemporaries. But this also meant that the currents and rocks around the island might not have been adequately charted and now, in the dark, they apprehensively negotiated their passage towards the island of Martin Vaz. Soon after this they saw their first albatross and finally passed out of home waters.

They lost the Trades at 22° South and entered a high-pressure zone. Here they were initially forced to go east rather than south, and soon found themselves being blown north by a southerly gale, the waves rising. They hove to and had dinner while the sea pitched violently around them. Soon after they got under way again they found themselves in a westerly gale, too strong to set their square sail. The wind shrieked in the rigging, the sea was a series of dark mountain ranges rising against the sky, and spurs of water exploded against the sides of the boat. It was almost impossible to steer. When the gale had blown itself out they got back on course only to encounter another.

Battered and exhausted they finally approached Cape Town. They changed into shore-going clothes and stripped the sails just as the harbour launch arrived to tow them – a deep-water ship – into harbour where crowds of Irish were, according to Lavelle, waiting 'to put their feet again on to what they called "a little bit of Ireland."' It was 6 October, four months since they had set sail from Dun Laoghaire.

Although Conor would be scathing about the colonies he could enjoy himself there. He stayed in Cape Town for two weeks and had a holiday. Making contact with local climbers he scaled Table Mountain, although the last five weeks afloat had left him with an unsettlingly precarious sense of balance. If to be a traveller is to enjoy the strangeness of new places, Conor was no traveller for he was constantly – reassuringly – reminded of home. The Cape was like southern England and, standing on Table Mountain looking out over the fantastically grooved and tunnelled rocks, he was reminded of the 'bare blue slabs of Aran' seen from Dún Aengus on Inis Mór. There were other yachts of *Saoirse*'s size in the harbour with owners who were keen to discuss yachting, and Conor enjoyed their company.

He left the supervision of repairs – the mast needed urgent treatment after the storms – to Lavelle and Hodge. He would regret this temporary lapse in his vigilance for they too wanted a break: Lavelle went fishing in mountain streams and spent a week motoring across the veldt. This meant more debts, and O'Brien, irritated and worried, itched to discharge them, but, again, did nothing. Gratifyingly for O'Brien, when they left Cape Town, *Saoirse*, now a celebrity, was towed out through a dense throng of vessels.

It was when they were out of Table Bay that O'Brien noticed that the forestay was loose. With rising anger, he checked the other repairs and found eight defects. He was furious. He had spent a large amount of money in Cape Town and had nothing to show for it except a new mast. He immediately set a course for Durban determined to discharge his crew. 'I tried to take a few days off duty in Capetown', he wrote to Dermod once he reached port, 'with the result that my crew, who seemed to have no idea beyond living gorgeously at my expense, allowed me to be so abominably swindled by bad workmen & dishonest traders that I had to put in here very much in distress, short of all kinds of provisions & a regular wreck, to discharge them'.[19]

It took two weeks to get to Durban. It was the worst sail of the journey for all trust had been wiped out. He had no doubts about how to treat them once they arrived in Durban:

> I expect Lavelle felt rather small though when he found a steerage ticket by the next boat shoved into his hand & he was told to get the hell out of it. He has probably spun a marvellous yarn to Miss Mackie about my brutal methods, but the fact is that the fellow is a sponge of the first order and hadn't even the grace to give me a word of

> thanks for the very good time I had given him …The other chap wasn't quite so unscrupulous about money, but he didn't do a hand's turn for the ship & besides was plainly incompetent. So he's gone too.[20]

O'Brien despised Hodge. But Lavelle had become a good sailor and O'Brien's anticipation of his reaction suggests that he felt more personally bound to him and was disappointed in his behaviour. O'Brien's anger was exorcised from his later account in *Across Three Oceans* and he blamed himself for not supervising the work in Cape Town. He also maintained that Lavelle and Hodge left of their own initiative. In fact O'Brien paid for both of them to get passages back to Ireland, though he made sure that the money was later refunded.

It would be a month before he would find another crew. He had lost time and money because of the repairs; now he had lost the men who had set out with him, and he would lose more time and money looking for replacements. His sense of overall control was being eroded and he had to adjust to the voyage as the management of the chronically unpredictable. He contemplated turning back. It seemed a sensible idea, but his desire to complete the voyage was stronger.

By early December he had signed on two ordinary seamen – Edward Chester and Henry Baker – from a boat that had been seized for debts. He did not trust them as sailors: 'I can see quite plainly that I'll have to superintend in person every mortal thing that's done about the ship from this out,' he told Dermod.

Just before he left Durban on 10 December he recruited a frightened teenage boy – Laurence Waterfall – who was eager to get away from a man posing as his father. Training the boy as a cook, steward and helmsman brought out the best in O'Brien. He liked him and regarded his faults, which were many, as the result of a bad upbringing; O'Brien felt he was the first person ever to have given Waterfall any focused attention. As the boy posed no threat to his authority, O'Brien could temper his aloofness and high standards with consideration and care. The boy responded well:

he became O'Brien's best helmsman, and when he got a job in Melbourne told O'Brien that he 'had made a man of him'. O'Brien felt some affection for him: 'my poor boy', he wrote, 'had a genius [for upsetting things].'

The other two men were the taciturn crew referred to earlier. When one-sided attempts at conversion failed O'Brien lapsed into unsociability. They did what they were told and never made the same mistake twice. 'It was like sailing a ship full of fool-proof machinery single-handed, a most restful occupation compared with the management of people who thought they could sail the ship too.'[21] But their impenetrability was profoundly disconcerting. O'Brien could not fathom their motives: did they fail to express opinions because they were easy going and well disciplined or because their pay was too low? And it was not clear why the elder refused a 50 per cent rise and the rating of bosun.

They sailed for two months from Durban to Melbourne across the Indian Ocean and the voyage was so comfortable that O'Brien forgot many of the details. After an initial fortnight of baffling winds they reached the thirty-sixth parallel on 21 December, just approaching the Roaring Forties. After that they had a steady westerly wind and did satisfying 140-nautical-mile daily runs for a week. This was one of many occasions when *Saoirse* recorded high average speeds with the wind behind her in the demanding waters of the Southern Ocean. They detoured south to Amsterdam Island partly to check the chronometer, but also because a ship-chandler's in Durban had sold O'Brien a chart and instructed him to look for shipwreck survivors. It was too foggy to anchor. They passed by and into a period of smooth seas in which O'Brien was able to undertake repairs to the ship.

O'Brien had expected to anchor at Littleton in Australia, but instead put into Williamstown, near Melbourne for much-needed supplies. It was 3 February 1924, the middle of the southern summer. The next day the crew deserted. They had left the ship to buy provisions, returned and gone to bed. When O'Brien went at dawn to wake the boy his hand met emptiness.

So were the other two bunks empty, and the boat [tender] was gone. A large trunk, a bag, and a coat or two were in evidence, so at first I supposed that my crew would come back before long, especially as none of them were very well provided with money. I had divided the total cash on board into five parts; one for each of us and one for the ship, and it was only £7 10s to begin with. Later in the morning I noticed that the bag had collapsed; I looked inside, and found it empty. The trunk was empty.[22]

O'Brien was, briefly, in shock. His professional relations with the crew had been good and, despite finding them impenetrable, he had never imagined that they would leave. And now that they had gone he knew that it was almost certain that he would not get to New Zealand in time to climb with his friends. His only recourse was to report the men as deserters and look for replacements.

Finding another crew was even more difficult than it had been in South Africa. *Saoirse*'s arrival at the port – a small, unknown yacht with an obviously serious purpose – was a noteworthy phenomenon. When it was known that O'Brien was heading for Cape Horn he became the object of curiosity.[23] It is not surprising that, inspired by the desertion, the local press was soon depicting the skipper of this strange yacht as a violent and threatening man.

In desperation O'Brien went to the shipping office for crew – he usually preferred to find his own crew – and was surprised by their promptness in presenting three Tasmanians. One day out of Melbourne revealed why: they had no idea how to sail a yacht. In *Across Three Oceans* O'Brien claimed that he purposefully found a headwind and difficult sea so that they would want to go back to Melbourne. At the time he told the press that he had merely asked them if they wished to continue after an episode of 'moderately heavy sea'. The crew opportunistically cast doubt on *Saoirse*'s ability to sail in rough seas: 'Even in a moderate sea the Saoirse moves violently, but her actions in heavy weather defy description.' This was after they had robbed him of a gold watch and the refunded money from

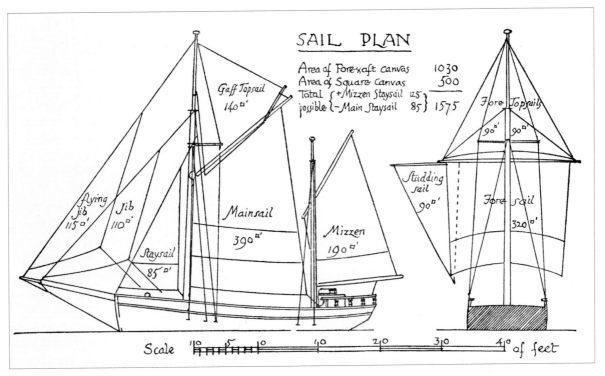

Saoirse sail plan drawn by O'Brien, published in *Across Three Oceans*.

Lavelle and Hodge.[24] Without a crew O'Brien was confined to his ship, and his opinion of Australians – never good because of his snobbishness about colonials – plummeted.

In compensation he received a cable from Dermod, and he met two yacht owners who gave him valuable advice. He participated in the Williamstown–Geelong race and *Saoirse* was photographed in full sail for the press. Finally he hired two companionable men. He liked both of them, but there were difficulties associated with each. 'G' (probably G. W. Green in the logbook) was Swedish–American, an affectionate 'soft slow man with a charming smile and imperturbable temper; a man brought up for the most part in five- and six-masted schooners, no doubt an excellent fellow to work all the gear of his mast with a steam capstan, but altogether too soft and slow for me.'[25] But a man whose company he enjoyed. 'W' (probably C. Willoughby in the logbook) was English. He was O'Brien's social equal and had a good record as an officer. Wiry, active, he was also nervous,

unpredictable and vulnerable. He had led an adventurous life and was now down and out. 'His temperament was too much like mine for safety, but I was prepared to risk a clash for the sake of having an educated Englishman to talk to.'[26] They proved, initially at least, to be a biddable and an emotionally robust crew: '[they are] not so damned touchy as that first lot and don't mind a bit of cursing when they know they deserve it.'[27]

O'Brien left Melbourne in high spirits telling Dermod that the ship was in first class order, the crew competent, and that he expected to call at one New Zealand port before going on to Rio de Janeiro. Australia, he thought, had merely been a calamitous interlude.

It was in fact only the beginning of a protracted nine-month hiatus in the journey. One night, three days out of Melbourne, O'Brien came as close to a sailing disaster as he was to get on this voyage when, blinded by the gas lights blazing in the cabin, they nearly ran into a great pyramid of black rock. 'Fortunately my mate was quick in action, the vessel quick on her helm, the wind off shore, and the water smooth, or the cruise would have ended then and there on Clarke Island.'

Not long after this Green knocked his elbow, which swelled up so badly that they had to stop at Picton on the north coast of New Zealand's South Island to find a doctor. He was in hospital for two weeks. They left Picton expecting Montevideo to be their next stop but within days the Englishman, Willoughby, hit his knee, which turned septic. They put in at Napier on the east side of North Island and O'Brien was told that Willoughby would be in hospital for a month.

It was now 10 May 1924 and the southern winter. The storms were incessant. They witnessed two gales and a flood in which houses slid down a hillside before their eyes. It would be impossible to set out for Cape Horn until the spring. This was the pivotal crisis of the voyage, for the extra months meant considerably more expenditure than had originally been calculated. There were potential ways of making money – he could go to Auckland and recruit paying passengers for a yachting or pearling trip around the islands – but the question that he began to address again in Napier was whether it was worth carrying on. He aired the pros and cons to Smith-Gordon:

> It seems a stupid thing after having spent so much on this voyage to chuck it up having achieved nothing; but its more stupid to throw good money after bad. The question is, shall I lose more by cutting my losses and coming home with my tail between my legs, or by trying to get on with the cruise? I am not very hopeful of getting much more by selling than will pay my expenses. Where I want your advice is on the question of what I stand to make if I do succeed in this enterprise.
>
> (a) You have probably read my article in the I.T. [Irish Times] As many more of those, filled out a bit (for some were written in a great hurry) would make a book. How much is that worth?
> (b) A more popular book will probably be called for. I hate popular books, but needs must

> when the devil drives; & I don't see why the movies shouldn't pay me something.
>
> Our dud government ought to do something for me (even if its only refunding the duty I paid in Dublin – alone of all ports [this rankled] – on my drinks and smokes) as I have carried the flag to 5 countries where it had never before been flown. But if I know them they won't. I have a perpetual and not always successful struggle to avoid getting classed as a British ship.

He told Smith-Gordon that he did not want to lose the crew who were both keen to go on, and that he had a month's worth of money to keep him going in Auckland. 'If it's a good gamble cable me there and I'll go on – I can do it, and the ship can do it – it's a question if you can.'[28]

His arguments were all in favour of going on and that last piece of rhetoric finally disclosed the real purpose of his letter as an appeal for money. O'Brien was very careful with the guarantees he had set out with (he refrained from drawing down money in Melbourne, waiting until he got to New Zealand) and, judging by the efforts he made to earn money in New Zealand, wanted to be as self-sufficient as possible. However, it was becoming increasingly obvious as the enforced delay in New Zealand lengthened that he was going to need extra funding from Ireland.

Just over a week later he was in Auckland where he wrote an unusually long letter to Dermod explaining his present circumstances.

> Well, this last accident [Willoughby's knee] has I am afraid wrecked the cruise altogether. I'm not in the least keen to start for the Horn at this time of the year, & have come to Auckland which is the most yachty port in New Zealand to try if I can get someone to finance a cruise round the islands; otherwise it looks very much like cutting my losses & selling the ship, which I feel would be a very mean thing to do. I have cabled to S-G [Smith-Gordon] & also written explaining the circumstances, the most salient of which is that if I can neither get a charter nor sell the ship

she will be seized for debt, in which case I shall get very little more out of it than my passage home. And if I can't keep this crew together, what chance have I of getting a new one? I'm just about tired of the worry of the whole thing, & wish to the Lord I had turned back from Durban, but having got this far I must make an effort to finish the job. The trouble is that there are not too many competent seamen around these days, & those that fail to get or to keep a better job than this one generally fail for a very obvious reason which makes them useless to me while the ship is in port. And so far I have been longer in port than at sea. As for getting any help, or indeed a day's work for a day's pay out of the natives of these parts – Well, you're always cursing the people at home, but wait till you try Australia!'

... One of the reasons why I have been rather slack about writing lately is that I didn't want to unload this continuous grouse & despondency onto people who have troubles enough of their own; but sooner or later the facts have got to come out, and I had better have the explaining of them. Perhaps it is the close quarters that makes it impossible to keep a crew; other small yachts that have done the same kind of thing have had the same experience. Except that with us things have gone all right as long as we were at sea.

... I wish I was back in Ireland again – I want desperately to see how things are getting on, though I gather they are not getting on much. If only I could find an honest (or sober) man here to leave in charge of the ship I'd come back and try to raise funds at home to complete the voyage with. Yours Conor.'[29]

Constantly returning to his predicament, writing down his worries and resolutions as they occur to him, it is the artless letter of someone with an all-consuming problem writing to a sympathetic correspondent. Yet even as he confided his problems with the crew to Dermod, Conor slightly underplayed the seriousness. Other small yachts did not all have the same problems as *Saoirse* for at Melbourne O'Brien had looked enviously at the *Seaweed*, a yacht about the same size as *Saoirse*,

which was sailed by a married couple and a man who had been with them from Southampton. And at sea the atmosphere on board *Saoirse* had rarely been entirely harmonious. The letter was not only written to vent his frustrations. Behind the descriptions and arguments there is the appeal again, not directly stated, for money.

Auckland would prove to be a difficult place in which to operate. O'Brien had had problems when he had first arrived merely getting noticed to complete ship's business. Without friends and contacts he found it impossible to arrange for a cruise and, reluctantly, he paid Green off. He tried hard but failed to sell *Saoirse*. When Willoughby returned to the ship, he was in an unsettled and fragile state. He had met up with some old friends and they seemed to be pushing the young man back into his old hopeless life. O'Brien, who had become fond of him, noticed this with sadness. O'Brien became very despondent. On 22 June he put his worries into a letter to Dermod:

My great anxiety is lest I should be left again without a crew when I want to start home again; otherwise I should have paid both off and laid up the ship & lived ashore till September. So I am nursing my mate most carefully: he is a splendid seaman but fearfully difficult to handle on shore. And all this means appalling expense. If I don't get the passengers it will take all the money I can raise to get me home. I ought to have turned back at Durban as I was very near doing, but now that I have got so far I feel it would be a pity to throw it all up.

This isn't I'm afraid a very cheerful letter, but I'm not feeling cheerful. The further I go the deeper I seem to get involved in trouble. Well, I hope your news is better than mine.[30]

The finale came a week later. On 1 July Conor telegraphed to Dermod announcing that he was leaving for Tonga the following week with two passengers: 'but they will not pay enough to cover expenses so must call on your guarantee.' The next day Smith-Gordon telegraphed Conor: 'Letter received have agreed with Dermod advance further

Conor O'Brien and Kioa. Photograph published in *Across Three Oceans*, 1926.

two hundred one hundred sent to-day persevere.'

Despite his troubles O'Brien liked New Zealand, comparing it to Ireland. He enjoyed the myriad inlets, channels and sounds of the coast around Picton, while the mountains with their virgin forests reminded him of Glengariff. He made some limited enquiries about co-operation for Dermod and Smith-Gordon, but was unable to leave *Saoirse* to investigate further. Noting the relationship between the native Maoris and settlers, he judged that they lived equally but apart, both groups vulnerable to the corrupting influence of less egalitarian colonies. Tonga he found exotic and he spent days investigating the reefs and marvelling at the size and colours of the flowers, birds, butterflies and fish, 'so brilliant that they illuminate the greyest day.'[31] He admired the equitable economic structure on Nukualofa where every man over sixteen was entitled to a lifetime lease of eight acres on payment of taxes and rent.

But Tonga was not a paradise for O'Brien. Willoughby went on strike and, with one of the passengers, abandoned O'Brien at Nukualofa, leaving *Saoirse's* dinghy on a reef where it was destroyed. There was no going back after that and O'Brien later paid him off at the consulate with a sense that he had failed this vulnerable man. On 1 September O'Brien returned to Auckland with a crew of three Tongans. Two would leave, but the third, who 'swore he would go to the end of the world with me' travelled in *Saoirse* back to Ireland.

This was Kioa, a young man with an English, (possibly, Conor speculated, Methodist) grandfather and a strict work ethic who was nevertheless reluctant to settle down to the business he would inherit from his uncle. Instead he had run away to sea several times where he had learnt to sail small boats. A bond of mutual affection immediately sprang up between Kioa and O'Brien. Kioa, full of enthusiasm for Tonga, related its history to a receptive O'Brien. Once on the ship O'Brien discovered that Kioa was a talented cook and a thoughtful and tidy steward. He was also keen to learn, and O'Brien instructed him in navigation and helmsmanship.

Kioa's greatest asset was his unobtrusive industry and an implicit understanding of his role. Towards the end of the voyage they were the only two on the ship.

> I shall not soon forget those beautiful mornings of my passage from Pernambuco to the Western Islands, when Kioa, my mate, and I kept no night watches; I usually woke before he did, or if not he was not at the wheel but roasting coffee for me or doing some work about the deck. I did not have to relieve a tired, blear-eyed man huddled up in oilskins among empty cocoa-mugs and burnt matches, but stepped out naked into the sun on a deck free from the offence which the night before always is to the dawn.[32]

It was far from an equal relationship, for although Kioa took the helm, O'Brien was solely responsible: 'I had achieved not the ideal two men in a boat, but one man and a cook, which is the lesser optimum'. Comfortable with this O'Brien gave Kioa his complete trust. It was essentially a master–servant relationship, but one founded on affection and mutual dependence. The success of his relationship with Kioa was a relief to O'Brien who felt inadequate for his inability to keep his crew.

One semi-skilled sailor was not sufficient for rounding Cape Horn and O'Brien took on two other men – J. Lynch and J. Mooney – both Irish, who, like so many of the people he employed, were temporarily escaping intolerable shore-lives and using the ship as an interlude of paid work.

Saoirse left Auckland on 22 October 1924 cleared for Montevideo. It was spring. It would take just over six weeks to get to the Falkland Islands on what O'Brien described as an 'entirely orthodox' passage. Sailing by the book was a reassuring discipline for O'Brien who crossed the fiftieth parallel on 24 November nervously. They had gone into 'the last stage of the progressive frightfulness with which the Southern Ocean threatens the voyager'. The Southern Ocean, part geographic, part psychological, part literary construct embodied all that he feared. The nadir of this anticipated experience would be the arrival at the fifty-sixth parallel, a place of notoriously difficult seas, strong winds and proximity to the ice of Antarctica.

Their descent south was punctuated by accidents with their gear. Once across the boundary-marking fiftieth, O'Brien, fearful of ice, insisted on a 48-hour routine of air- and sea-temperature monitoring. Approaching doom seemed to be marked by the appearance of a new breed of albatross with the woolly coat of a sheep. Snow threatened. The wind dropped and the sea, which had been a deep sparkling blue, turned a dull and ugly black and the light drained from the sky. Without the breeze *Saoirse* became the plaything of violent currents pushing and pulling in all directions, so that the ship rolled and pitched alarmingly, while the sails slammed and the gear creaked. It was a relief when the wind, ice cold from the glaciers, returned, allowing O'Brien to lay his course and take control of the ship. So they proceeded through the thick and gloomy weather, cautiously keeping their distance from the shore and the multitude of islands that make up the cape. Then, as they approached the tip, the clouds lifted and the sun shone brightly. They could see great slopes of ice in the distance, and closer at hand they passed a succession of cliffs: the black cliffs of Hoste Island, the jagged outline of Hermite Island and finally the steep black cone of Cape Horn itself, not a cape but an island, named after a Dutchman.

It was when they got round to Staten Island on the east that they decided not to continue for distant Montevideo but to stop at the much nearer Falkland Islands. They dropped anchor in Port Stanley on 6 December. O'Brien sent a telegram to his sister Margaret, and on 18 December it was reported in the Irish press that *Saoirse* had rounded Cape Horn without accident 'and that Mr O'Brien has performed a feat which very few yachtsmen would dare to undertake'.

Isolation made the Falkland Islanders friendly towards visitors, and O'Brien allowed himself to be taken in charge. Within a short time the governor had instructed the Seal Protection Cruiser to show O'Brien penguins and seals, which he described at length in a letter to Margaret. Later he went in a mail steamer with the Colonial Secretary to the South Shetlands on the northernmost tip of Antarctica to investigate a Scottish whale factory. Here he saw ice, tabular and recently carved from nearby glaciers, recently capsized, peaked, and floe, the frozen surface of the sea. O'Brien and the crew were overwhelmed by offers of hospitality for Christmas. And because the Falkland Islands were so small he could rely on the authorities to help him supervise the crew. However, that did not prevent one from getting married and staying behind. The islanders' friendliness made his stay in the Falklands feel like a homecoming and the few planned weeks extended to three relaxed summer months.

Towed by HMCS *Afterglow* out of Port Stanley on 28 February 1925 O'Brien felt he had almost completed the voyage, for after the long months in the Pacific to be sailing in the Atlantic felt like a return to home waters. Subtly but undeniably O'Brien's relationship with *Saoirse* had altered, for as she survived her successive difficulties she wrought herself ever more tightly into O'Brien's soul. Ironically this coincided with an appreciation of her monetary value: as she became more sellable it was less likely that O'Brien would part from her.

The last leg of the voyage was not without incident. One of the crew who had been irritating O'Brien for months, began to complain of boils (Kioa had boils too but did not complain). He did less and less work until O'Brien decided to alter course for Pernambuco to get rid of him.

On 6 March, before he reached the port, O'Brien saw patches of kelp that he thought denoted an uncharted submerged rock. He reported it as a potential danger area to the British Consul in Pernambuco who suggested he contact the Navy hydrographer.[33] The hydrographer asked the Colonial Office to instruct a research cruiser in the South Atlantic to investigate. The outcome was not the naming of a submerged island (Saoirse Rock) but the identification of 'discoloured water', probably caused by a patch of seaweed.[34]

Leaving Pernambuco O'Brien found that his vision was seriously damaged: he could not see the buoys marking the channel, nor the detail on the chart; he could not read. He was suffering from snow or sun blindness, exacerbated, he thought, by not wearing dark glasses in Pernambuco. He only had Kioa now (promoted to mate) for the relatively easy journey through the Trades. But Kioa too was suddenly taken sick. Unable to read the small print in his medical book, O'Brien made a wrong diagnosis and thought that Kioa was about to die. Trying to conceal from Kioa that he was navigating largely by guesswork he brought the ship to Horta on the island of Faial in the Azores and got Kioa into hospital. While Kioa was being treated O'Brien asked his sister, the 'stalwart and reliable'[35] Kitty, to come out and help sail the boat home.

As he waited O'Brien wandered, half-blind, about Horta, a small place with grass growing in the main street. He was charmed by the beauty of the whitewashed Portuguese-style buildings (though he knew that the cleanliness and prettiness were confined to the fronts) and by the female telegraph clerks (most of them married, he told Margaret) who had the latest news from Valentia and Derrynane. It made him feel close to home. At ease he sat down to write a long letter to Margaret full of amusing stories.

The final leg of the journey started on 3 June 1925 with the comforting presence of Kitty aboard the ship. However, they were under pressure for O'Brien had told his friends in Dublin that he would sail on 1 June and they had set the arrival date for 20 June, exactly two years since he had first set sail. They approached Ireland in frustratingly light winds, but soon they were nearing Wicklow Head where Margaret joined them, and on 19 June anchored off Dalkey Island so that *Saoirse* could enter Dun Laoghaire Harbour on cue.

The reception was spectacular: about 10,000 people, the yachts of the three Irish yacht clubs hung with bunting and flags to accompany *Saoirse* into the basin, an aeroplane flying low over the ships, a band and a maroon signal from the pier head.[36] O'Brien emerged in dark glasses. He was cheered and carried shoulder-high as people pressed around. He was met by members of the Dun Laoghaire Urban District Council and then driven into Dublin in a procession of 100 motor cars headed by one carrying a model of *Saoirse* with his young godson, Conor Cruise O'Brien, dressed in a white sailor suit posing as Conor. That evening the Arts Club hosted a gala dinner. 'These things have nothing to do with the voyage, but show an appreciation of it for which I am deeply thankful,' he later wrote.[37]

The Irish Times depicted O'Brien as an ambassador for the new state, carrying the flag to places where it was unknown. It was the most noted voyage of the 1920s in yachting circles. O'Brien was awarded the Royal Cruising Club's Challenge Cup for the three years he had been away; an unprecedented accolade. The cruise made O'Brien's name.

O'Brien's family would regard the circumnavigation as beginning and ending at Foynes. His nephew Murrogh, then six, still remembers the tar barrels being dragged up the hill on Foynes Island so that a magnificent bonfire would greet O'Brien as he sailed up the Shannon Estuary a week later.

Chapter 9
Ilen

O'Brien started to write his book on the voyage – *Across Three Oceans*: *A Colonial Voyage in the Yacht 'Saoirse'* – shortly after he returned to Foynes Island. He finished it on 11 January 1926.[1] He had a contract with the publishers Edward Arnold in London: he was to get a good advance of £50 and a generous royalty of 20 per cent. They published it in 1926, illustrated with some of O'Brien's technical drawings and photographs from the voyage, and with an introduction by the veteran yacht cruiser, Claud Worth.

O'Brien did well out of it financially. It was a best-seller; there was a second impression in 1927, and another in 1928.[2] He revised it for a second edition in 1931. By then he had read widely about ocean yachting and was dubious about the accuracy of some of the conclusions he had drawn in 1927 and about the moments when he had adopted a didactic tone.[3]

Writing his account of the voyage Conor had been inspired by the descriptions of his cruising contemporaries and Joseph Conrad's success in telling 'the truth about the sea'.[4] Although he was predictably reticent about his personal life and minimised the risks, he was candid about their sailing experience and, keeping close to his log, took his readers through the convoluted operations of the many episodes of the voyage. For the non-sailor it is not a light read, although O'Brien tried to compensate for the inevitable technicalities with entertaining stories and descriptions of places and wildlife, and his oblique tone and elliptical

sentences – often witty, though sliding on occasions into obscurity – give the book a welcome edge. But his prime audience was the sailor and, perhaps even more pertinently, the would-be sailor who relished details about flying jibs, foresails and northeasters, and the vivid evocation of the sea in its many moods.

O'Brien returned from the circumnavigation with the idea that he might make some money designing and selling boats. He was proud of *Saoirse*'s speed, safety and her behaviour in challenging ocean conditions: 'I wanted every one to fall down and worship her, and those who were looking for new yachts to copy her design.'[5] He gave her a coat of paint, disguised any damage and took her on a publicity tour in which he emphasised the efficiency of the ship and the ease of the voyage. It was, he claimed, a complete failure. Those who were building yachts already knew what they wanted, and the general public, he discovered, would have preferred to hear about damage and hardship. And next to English ships that were finished with brass, silver and rare woods, *Saoirse* looked like a country cousin.

However, there had been expressions of interest in commissioning a ship from him during his circumnavigation. The Tongans wanted a copra cutter, and the manager at Darwin in the Falkland Islands had told him they were looking for a new boat to service the islands. The Darwin pilot, who would sail the new boat, had even confided that he would like *Saoirse* with an engine. The commission for the latter came by chance in typical O'Brien fashion when he went to change a Falkland pound at the Falkland Island Company headquarters in London and was passed from the cashier to the Company Secretary who was interested in O'Brien's experience and later recommended him

The *Ilen*, *Saoirse*'s larger cousin, tied alongside the coal store at Hegarty's Boatyard Quay, Oldcourt, County Cork, on the Ilen River, summer 2000.

Tom Moynihan and his men building *Ilen* at the Fisheries School, Baltimore, County Cork, 1925.

Ilen being launched with the assistance of Fishery School pupils, Baltimore, County Cork, 1926.

as the designer of a new boat.

Having already discussed the requirements of a boat to ferry people, live animals and stores between the islands in the often severe conditions of the South Atlantic, O'Brien, with Tom Moynihan of Baltimore, County Cork, confidently designed a new ship. It was similar to *Saoirse*, but narrower, shallower, and a more elegant 56 feet, 'with the long easy lines that ought to make for speed.' Building started in October 1925.

Because he was busy with *Across Three Oceans*, O'Brien did not have time to supervise the construction. The result was that he was dissatisfied with the details, particularly the propeller, clutch, and the engine, 'a sweet little thing, made by Bolinders', which was badly installed. *Ilen*, named after the river that runs into the sea at Baltimore, was registered in 1926.

There were the usual problems finding crew.

In the end he signed up two cousins from a family that owned and manned many of the schooners and ketches of Cape Clear Island, near Baltimore. As there was a slump in hiring such boats for transportation the crews were laid up. Denis Cadogan wanted experience in a foreign-going vessel to qualify as a second mate, while Con Cadogan wanted adventure before settling down as a farmer. They were hard working but Conor found Con inscrutable and disappointingly lacking in interest.[6]

They started their journey south in October 1926, just over three years since O'Brien had set out on the circumnavigation. It was very different from the previous voyage that, in retrospect, had been made in almost ideal circumstances in which the Southern Ocean had been well behaved and there had been no 'inconveniently fresh Trade winds'.[7] Now the winds were unpredictable

Ilen, built in 1926 at Baltimore Fisheries School, County Cork, seen here in 1948 anchored off Georgia Island, one of the Falkland Islands. *Ilen* remained in use in the Falklands until 1998 when she was repatriated.

Ilen sailing in Dublin Bay prior to her return trip to Baltimore, June 1998.

(l to r) Con Cadogan, Conor O'Brien and Dennis Cadogan in Bristol at the start of *Ilen*'s voyage to Port Stanley, 1926.

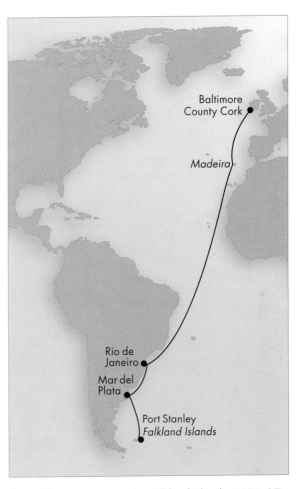

Ilen's delivery voyage to the Falkland Islands, 1926–27.

and the ship gave constant trouble. And, with a delivery deadline and an auxiliary engine and thus a reasonable chance of meeting the deadline without going out of their way, they did not have the luxury of looking for a fair wind and responding to circumstances. They stopped at Funchal and Pernambuco where they got introductions to authorities down the coast. They motored into Rio and O'Brien was horrified by a monstrous hotel behind Copacabana beach. After they left Rio they ran into a storm when, for a time, O'Brien feared they would drown.

The storm was prefigured by a threatening school of whales swimming high in the water. Then, 600 miles from Stanley and 10 days before Christmas, they were enveloped in a gloomy fog and felt a 'chill blast' from the south. Soon they were smashing pitilessly into high seas. They brought sufficient coal, food and water aft for two days, pumped the ship dry, hove to and gathered around the cabin stove, distracting themselves with stories of other gales. However, they were soon soaked with water squirting through holes around the skylight. Then there was an extra bad lurch, a bang, and the thunder of slatting canvas that

shook the whole ship. O'Brien jumped for the wheel and put the ship hard up, while Con and Denis at the other end of the ship dealt with the split staysail and its smashed gear. When they had finished O'Brien lashed the helm and went below to encourage the stove.

In a lull they heard water in the engine-room. The pump was choked, and they had to bale out, forming what felt like a useless chain of buckets against the great flood of water that was pouring in. Within an hour it was under control and they took a break. It was then that O'Brien panicked. Was there a leak? Could they keep baling for as long as the storm lasted? Could they keep afloat till it was fine enough to launch the boat? Did the boat and her oars still exist? If they did have a boat could they get

Ilen being discharged by dockers in Dublin's Alexandra Basin after a rough trip from Port Stanley, Falkland Islands, 1998.

Ilen's builder's plaque.

Ilen sailing into the bay of Baltimore on her return to her place of origin, 1998.

200 miles to the nearest land without a sail? 'Then I wondered what the other two were thinking about it, for nobody had spoken. And last I wondered what happened to one in the Hereafter … And then it was time to start baling again'. The action reduced his panic, and later that night he managed to doze on the sodden rags of his bed. When he woke in the morning the gale had moderated; there was no leak and he was able to get the pump working.

They made a detour to Argentinian Mar del Plata to celebrate Christmas. After a delay they set out again for Stanley, arriving on 8 January. *Ilen* was sold to Port Stanley on 16 April 1927.

Barneen, Foynes Island. Photograph taken in 2007.

Chapter 10
Foynes Island

When Conor went back to Ireland in 1927 it was to Foynes Island. Conor loved the estuary at this point where the land – low hills cut into fields – holds back from the river, and clouds tower over it. Sailing home from the mouth of the estuary he would enter the narrow sound between the steep wooded cliffs of Foynes and Barneen Point on the island. Here stood the single-storey house where he now lived. A former herdsman's cottage that had been converted by Sir Stephen de Vere in the 1880s, it had a simple porch and a narrow, timber-sheeted room almost filled by a hinged table that Conor had made and installed. In this room, with a view down the estuary and across the sound towards Charlotte Grace's house, Conor did much of his writing. It was reminiscent of *Saoirse*'s cabin: confined and timber-lined, economically accommodating.

Conor would land on the island at a small stone pier opposite Foynes village. From there he could choose whether to turn left to the solitary and spartan pleasures of Barneen or right, down a path overshadowed by mature trees to many-chimneyed, gabled and bay-windowed Monare, where Margaret and Hugh lived with nine-year-old Elinor and eight-year-old Murrogh in more patrician comfort.[1] Both houses are still there. Monare, an outpost of Victorianism, stands solidly, secure and hidden. Barneen, immediately visible, and vernacular in style, seems an emblem for the island. Below the path to Monare is a boathouse. This too is intact, and inside is a rowing dinghy built by Conor, its ribs and curves beautifully symmetrical, perfectly visible from the sound. This direct view straight into the boathouse is strangely compelling. It is as if O'Brien and his contemporaries on the island are still there and the boat is waiting to be launched to take them over to Foynes.

Cooking, making furniture and boats, Conor led a self-sufficient, practical and ordered life on Foynes Island, not dissimilar to his life on board *Saoirse*. Apart from the fourteen-foot rowing boat, he also built a sailing dinghy for the family to use getting to and from the mainland.[2] He made a virtue of the fact that there was no power on the island, and enjoyed working by hand. Fortunately his relationship with his family did not mirror that with his crew, but he could maintain a distance and detachment, sometimes arriving late for a meal and then hardly speaking.[3] A photograph of Conor and Margaret standing outside the porch he constructed on Barneen gives an insight into the relaxed complicity of the brother and sister. Similar in height, they stand companionably in equally creased cotton summer working clothes; Margaret in an improvised dress with a leather belt and bulging pockets, and leggings, Conor in open-necked shirt and shorts and a belt identical to his sister's.

Conor's practical self-sufficiency can be related to the vogue for the Arts and Crafts, which, in Britain at least, continued well into the twentieth century, becoming ever more focused on the domestic. O'Brien though was not being modish. He was merely translating the beliefs and tastes that had shaped the making of *Saoirse* and governed his life on board into his life with his family. If O'Brien had related his way of living to a broader concept in the late 1920s he was more likely to think in terms of islands. Island communities at that time were by nature isolated and by necessity self-reliant and independent-minded, for that which came from the mainland had been transported with some difficulty in small boats. Their life revolved around making the best use of what was to hand.

Living in the west of Ireland also had another resonance in the 1920s. The west, particularly the far

Conor O'Brien with his sister Margaret outside Barneen, Foynes Island in 1913.

Barneen, Foynes Island c. 1900.

west, had been regarded since the late nineteenth century as the mythic cradle of Irish civilisation and the place where an authentic Gaelic Ireland could be rediscovered. In the early years of the Free State this idea had become a cultural commonplace.[4] Even realist writers such as Liam O'Flaherty who knew the west well were not immune to its mythic resonance. Conor may not have romanticised Foynes Island in this way, but with his knowledge of Irish and his empathy for the hard, physical life of rural communities, he would have appreciated the particular quality of the life that the island offered. Although a significant number of Protestants had travelled to western islands in search of primeval Ireland, very few had lived there. By centring their lives on the island Conor and his sister's family were also implicitly underlining the authentic Irish credentials of the O'Briens.

Conor worked with Michael and John Finucane on the island. He observed people he came into contact with carefully: farmers, fishermen, boat-builders, people who had returned from America,

people whose families had run shops and pubs for several generations and, as the port grew at Foynes and the flying boats arrived, dock and port workers. In *The Runaways* O'Brien drew an affectionate portrait of 'Mr Moriarty'. There is a hint of the Irish stereotype in his eccentricity and contrariness, but the portrait is specific enough to be based on a real character.

Mr Moriarty was standing in the doorway of a small house a little back from the quay, where he could see everything that moved in Callamore. He was an enormous man, and the doorway was very narrow; if there were any secrets behind his broad back they would stay hidden. He wore a tail-coat and trousers of the striking black-and-white diamond pattern affected by Kerry homespun weavers, and a wide black low-crowned hat covered his white hair. You would take him for a retired seaman rather than a shopkeeper, and you would be right. What he didn't know about sailing-vessels wasn't worth knowing; but when he lost his job in sail he didn't go into steam. He just hung about, gossiping with such other old sailors as came into the port and ruminating over old times as he handled the piles of junk which he had collected more as souvenirs than as merchandise. He wasn't registered as a marine-store dealer, nor a pawnbroker, and he had never been accused of receiving stolen goods; he was far too careful about his customers. If you came to him with good introductions he gave you a very square deal, as temporarily impecunious Naval officers knew well; if you hadn't the introduction he wouldn't deal at all.

Conor appreciated the details of his clothing and was fascinated by the subversive ambivalence of his self-appointed position. Perhaps he also identified with men such as these who remained sturdily aloof to changes in fashion and technology and who managed to earn an income doing what they enjoyed on their own terms.

In 1925 Conor made a bid for a seat in the Senate. He had set out on his circumnavigation a month after the truce that had called a halt to the Civil War. When he returned Cumann na nGaedhael (the Free State party) had been in undisputed power for two years. The Senate, the upper house of the Oireachtas (legislature), was one of the few institutions that made provision for Protestants.[5] In a country that was heavily influenced by the socially conservative Catholic hierarchy, the Senate was proving to be the one place where a more liberal agenda could be debated. Conor hoped to further the interests of the fishing industry. So far it had been undervalued: when the first Free State minister for fisheries had been appointed at the end of 1922 his role was only administrative, and from 1924 fisheries had been amalgamated with rural industries.

In his press statement O'Brien outlined his family's achievements and listed his own credentials: fluent Irish speaker, original member of Sinn Féin and the Gaelic League, architect, strong adherent of co-operation, involved in gunrunning,

circumnavigator, writer on navigation and the mercantile marine, inspector of fisheries. His celebrity as a yachtsman – limited, yet, in certain circles, potent – failed to glamorise him sufficiently to counteract the politically unfashionable fisheries and his Protestant background, and he was not elected.

His failure to get elected was a reflection of the lack of recognition that was given to his sailing achievements in Ireland. This was not true at the time of his circumnavigation for, as we have seen, he had extensive coverage from *The Irish Times* and the *Irish Independent* on his departure and return. But by his death in 1952 only *The Irish Times* with its largely unionist, Anglo-Irish and liberal readership, gave him a generous obituary. The populist *Independent* merely included his death in the list that filled the front page in those days. The Free State cultivated Gaelic games and had little time for a sport that was associated with the Ascendancy. For remuneration and recognition O'Brien had to look to England, and it is only very recently that the sailing achievements of Irish men and women have been appreciated beyond the yacht clubs.[6]

In 1927 O'Brien entered *Saoirse* in the Fastnet Race. It was the third year of a race, instituted in 1925, which would become one of the classic biennial offshore races. It was a gruelling 608 miles, linking sociable Cowes with Fastnet, which stands alone in the ocean off the south-west coast of Ireland, a lighthouse grafted onto the side of a vast rock, like a ship headed for America. The boats set off from Cowes, sailed around Fastnet Rock and returned to Plymouth in unpredictable and sometimes dangerous weather.

1927 was particularly inclement. Conor's crew included the writer and sailor, Maurice Griffiths and his wife Peter, Conor's sister, Kitty and several others. Griffiths has left a lively account of the race, which started off in mist, a south-west wind rising. 'As *Saoirse* rolled and lurched in the gathering seas past the Bembridge Ledge buoy and out into the gloom of the Channel the double note of the Nab Tower foghorn followed us, plaintive and thin through the driving rain, and I can even now clearly hear the doleful two tone *whee-whaw* above the wash of the seas and the occasional shudder from aloft as the square topsail luff shook in the wind.'[7] Griffiths found *Saoirse* a strange ship: there were more ropes than he was used to, her hull seemed a bit short and her bowsprit rather long. With darkness the weather deteriorated and he became sick as *Saoirse* bucked, her bowsprit 'alternatively [stabbing] the sky and the face of the next oncoming comber.' But after a night of slow and steady progress through a force 8 wind he was describing *Saoirse* as a 'game little ship', a 'tough little vessel'. O'Brien, though, realised that that was not enough. 'After twenty-four hours we were having a hot race for last place with the smallest boat in the fleet.'[8] Thirteen of the fifteen entries, including *Saoirse*, turned back before they reached Fastnet Rock. O'Brien enjoyed the camaraderie of the race, but he knew that many who entered had never sailed in the Atlantic, and he criticised the organisers for being irresponsibly amateur not to insist that crews should have prior experience of the voyage.

He spent much of his time in late 1927 and early 1928 writing. *From Three Yachts*, an account of his experiences in *Kelpie, Saoirse* and *Ilen,* was commissioned by the publisher of *Across Three Oceans* and was obviously designed to capitalise on its success. Keen to present his particular view of sailing to a knowledgeable audience he adopted a slightly combative though disarmingly frank tone. He began by chastising those who expect adventures and stories – 'yarns' – from sailors, and by emphasising the importance of safety and comfort: 'To make any sort of a story … one must yacht dangerously; and the fact that I find it hard to dig a few dangerous, or even strenuous, incidents out of my log-books proves that cruising can be, and to my mind should be, an easy and luxurious life.' He contributed articles to *Yachting Monthly*, keeping up a 'provocative and delightful' correspondence with Maurice Griffiths, who was its editor.[9]

He wrote two thrillers, but was unable to get them published.[10] This attempt suggests that he had discovered a desire to write and wished to experiment; that he was beginning to see himself as a writer.

In April 1928 he was staying at St Anthony, Porthscatho, a village popular with yachtsmen on the southern coast of Cornwall, where his sister Kitty had a house and where he could berth *Saoirse*. From here he wrote a letter to Dermod that tentatively revolved around a new interest: he was thinking of getting married.

Chapter 11
Marriage

It is a measure of the painter Kitty Clausen's love for Conor, as well as the compatibility of their tastes, and her adaptability, that she was able to take on *Saoirse* and what had become Conor's intermittently nomadic way of life. Unfortunately Kitty has left relatively little behind. Only one of her letters is available so far. There are no diaries or journals. Conor wrote about her, but sparsely and in an oblique and indirect way.

She died young and a friend from her student days, Una Hook, wrote a tribute to her in *The Times*.[1] This woman wanted to convey the delight she had felt in Kitty's presence and wrote of her sparkling personality, her 'charm of sterling worth'. She described Kitty's wide circle of friends in all walks of life 'among whom her bright presence was known and her untiring kindness and her interest felt.' Behind words that speak eloquently of the too-early loss of a friend there is the sense of a woman who attracted people to her because of her interest in and empathy for them. Where Conor could be choosy, reserved, discriminating, difficult, Kitty seems to have been open, accepting, considerate. These qualities ran through her personality and her encounters; veins in a rock rather than veneer or polish. Conor and Kitty may have been significantly different but they both seem to have been people who were true to themselves.

Katharine Frances Clausen was the daughter of Sir George Clausen (he was knighted in 1927), one of the foremost English painters of landscape and rural life of his day. Like the designers of the Arts and Crafts movement he was passionately interested in recording the rapidly disappearing rural traditions of the late nineteenth and early twentieth century. Influenced by French *plein air* painters such as Bastien Lepage, he tried to represent the ever-changing qualities of sunlight and shade in rural scenes, and his reputation was founded on his success in this. He taught at the Royal Academy where he gave well-received lectures and influenced the next generation, not least his own daughter.[2]

Born in 1886 (she was six years younger than Conor) Kitty was brought up in a comfortable middle class home in Carlton Hill, St John's Wood, a part of London that was colonised by artists and writers at that time (described in retrospect by Evelyn Waugh in *Work Suspended*). She was the youngest of three girls and also had two brothers, one of whom, Hugh, was a temporary officer in the RNVR. He would become an engineering design consultant and occasional crew of *Saoirse*. She first attended the Royal Academy in July 1908 and stayed five years, winning prizes for figure painting in 1910 and 1911, and extending her studies by winning the Landseer Scholarship (worth a considerable £40) in 1911.[3] When the war broke out she became a nurse, working at home and abroad. She spent her spare time drawing whatever was at hand, honing her observational and technical skills.[4] Portraits and still life, particularly flowers, were her subjects, judging by her entries to the Royal Academy Summer Exhibition where she began exhibiting in 1915. After a show at the Goupil Gallery in London she went to Italy and was inspired by the colour and light which, according to one critic, 'made [her art] blossom into a wholly unexpected beauty, the beauty of outward appearances and their spiritual significance.' It also left her with a desire to go back south to paint.

Conor O'Brien and his wife Kitty Clausen on board *Saoirse* in the 1930s.

In 1920, aged 34, Kitty either left home or rented a studio a few roads away from Carlton Hill, moving to West London in 1927. Judging by a surviving letter to her parents she remained close to them: she was chatty and affectionate and signed herself 'Kit'.[5] She was working (and possibly living) in West London when she first knew Conor, an independent woman of 39, established in a moderately successful career as a painter. She received commissions for portraits, exhibited at the Royal Watercolour Society, the New English Art Club, and the Fine Art Society, and had the support, encouragement and approval of her father.[6]

She was tall, about Conor's height, and slim, about seven stone according to Conor. Her one surviving letter to her parents is written in a quick, round, messy hand, suggesting spontaneity. She has underlined words for emphasis, as though speaking. Running her sentences together with '&s' suggests that she spoke quickly, that with her parents at least she was confident of an attentive audience. She had short hair, sometimes cut in a fashionable bob, or she wound a scarf about her head, turban-style. There are no available photographs of her before she married Conor, but two taken afterwards show her in practical working clothes: tweed trousers, a roll-neck jumper, a shirt with the sleeves pulled up. One of the photographs shows her working with Conor on *Saoirse*, raising a sail. Conor, better placed to be effective, is putting in more effort, but Kitty looks the part in her worn clothes, and the photograph conveys a robust impression of joint effort and mutual support.

It is likely that Conor met Kitty through Dermod who had known Sir George and his family since at least early 1917.[7] They certainly knew each other by 1927 when Kitty drew a pastel portrait of Conor.[8] The drawing shows a rugged 47-year-old Conor smoking a small cigar. He holds himself in reserve but there is a watching interest in the eyes that look at the artist and out at the viewer. The hand that holds the cigar is huge. It is a good portrait, full of the personality of the sitter.

Women, apart from his sisters, do not seem to have played a very significant role in Conor's life before he met Kitty and he seems to have been reticent with them. He was certainly not the man to reveal his feelings about Kitty to Dermod, but he did ask his brother for advice about the marriage. Dermod replied promptly, and in the letter of 11 April 1928 from Cornwall Conor responded, referring obliquely to the possibility of marriage without mentioning Kitty's name. The ostensible subject of the letter was a projected voyage to Brazil in June.[9]

> … *the right kind of wife, though she believes in the literary value of my work, has grave doubts about its commercial value, even when embellished with her own illustrations. So the personnel of the Brazilian voyage is at the moment uncertain. It consists definitely of two very young & I think very nice Cambridge undergraduates, who are paying their own expenses but [are] unable to contribute anything to the ship.*

At the end of the letter he tells Dermod that he has finished another thriller which looks more marketable than 'No 1' being more competent, though not so interesting. 'It may make the right sort of wife a practical proposition.'

One suspects that Conor felt he was in no financial position to marry and that his initial request to Dermod had been about money and prospects. Equally one suspects, though with less evidence (except the forthrightness, possibly playful, which claimed to have 'grave doubts' about the commercial value of his writing), that Kitty was not worried about O'Brien's ability to support her. She came from a comfortable background and was living independently. Conor's light tone to Dermod suggests that his own concerns would ultimately be flimsy doubts, which affection and friendship would disperse.

The Clausens liked Conor. After his visit to their country house in Essex in the late summer of 1928 Sir George relayed his feelings to Dermod. '… we all like him very much indeed. I was impressed with his clear-headed wisdom (though I believe he's considered impracticable) and Kitty is quite of the same mind, so we think them well suited to each other.'

They were married on 10 October 1928 in St Martin's Church, Hamilton Terrace, around the corner from Carlton Hill. Kitty immediately adopted *Saoirse* so that their Christmas card that year depicted a golden sailing boat on a black background under which was a handwritten and disarmingly self-satisfied verse:

> May the small ship depicted here
> Full freighted with our happiness
> Convey our wish for this new year
> That your content may be no less.[10]

Conor had at last found someone with whom he could share *Saoirse* on equal terms. In his book on the voyage they made to the Mediterranean in 1931–2, in which Kitty was the mate, he several times paid homage to her seamanship which he described romantically as deriving from her special affinity with *Saoirse*.

> That we anchored safely in Alicante is due jointly to the mate and to the ship. There is a mutual confidence between them which I, who have known the ship so much longer, do not share. But then, if I have entire confidence in my wife, that comes to the same thing. She is, for both of us, the perfect crew. When the present articles, in which she is falsely described as cook, expire, she shall sign at full A.B.'s [able seaman's] wages on the new ones. She earned them in that dreadful week we spent coming from Cartagena![11]

For Kitty to be the perfect crew was the highest accolade, and perhaps, given O'Brien's identification with *Saoirse*, it was also an expression of his joy in Kitty's understanding of him.

The idea that Kitty's intuition made up for her lack of experience owes something to the stereotype of women reliant on instinctive ability and understanding. Yet the impression from the glimpses of their life aboard *Saoirse* is that they lived as equals. They took turns at the helm and Kitty did her share of the rough work. In the letter written to her parents on 2 April 1934 from Ibiza

Kitty Clausen on the deck of *Saoirse*.

Kitty describes her part in helping to haul *Saoirse* onto the slip to scrape barnacles from her bottom prior to giving her a coat of antifouling paint: 'we are all rather stiff & tired with washing and scraping'. She was, Conor wrote, 'as good as a man within the limitation of her seven stone odd weight, and a lucky hand at the wheel.'[12] Conor, aware of his impatience – 'my besetting sin is hastiness' – valued Kitty's more laid-back approach. If they were caught in a fog or undesirable wind Conor was always tempted to go in the wrong direction to look for better conditions while Kitty counselled patience: wait for the fog to lift or the wind to change direction. He compensated for his superior knowledge by not laying down the law, while she compensated for her inexperience with rigorous discipline. Both planned to work when they came to harbour: Kitty to paint, Conor to write. Both sent their work to London to galleries and publishers.

Together they domesticated *Saoirse*.

Conor O'Brien sitting on the deckhouse of *Saoirse* in the Mediterranean c. 1934.

Christmas card from Conor and Kitty, 1928, featuring *Saoirse*.

During the first three years of her existence *Saoirse* had been regarded primarily as a means of transport, and because rapid transport by sea is not compatible with comfort except in the very largest liners, and her crews were chosen rather with a view to efficiency of transport … than to congeniality, she was lacking in those amenities of a home which are the essence of yachting. I had myself forgotten this aspect so far that I thought about nothing except times and speeds, courses and distances, and talked and wrote of winds and currents and the approved routes of sailing vessels to the infinite boredom of my hearers and readers.[13]

In the tranquil harbours of the Mediterranean they could inhabit the cabin: hang the clock that Kitty's brother Hugh Clausen had given them for a wedding present, lay down a locally woven rug, store plates on a wall shelf, prop a case of paints against a bench seat, put flowers in a jug and scatter books on the central table.[14] All this is lovingly recorded in a pastel of Kitty's which was reproduced in *Voyage and Discovery*. O'Brien is at the centre, engrossed in his work, but it is entitled 'The Exercise of our Respective Trades', and the presence of the invisible artist is palpable, for there is a box of paints leaning tidily against a built-in seat at the edge of the picture. Even in a storm *Saoirse* was well behaved now, the cabin so quiet that the noise of a teacup with a slightly roughened handle, which grated on the hook from which it was hung, was disturbingly loud.

Kitty never quite got over her seasickness sailing around the Irish coast so they decided to sail south for better weather. O'Brien had re-rigged *Saoirse* as a true square-rigger in 1927. (He added a

A shirtless Conor O'Brien propelling his engineless *Saoirse* around Ibiza Harbour, 1931. Resourceful as ever, in very light conditions O'Brien could propel *Saoirse* along at 1¼ knots with the use of a 19-foot yuloh. This was an oriental type of sweep or sculling oar.

Saoirse running before an Atlantic gale off the Portugese coast c. 1931. Pastel by Kitty Clausen with the contemporary photograph on which it was based inset. The pastel was published in *Voyage and Discovery,* 1933.

square sail and twin foretopsails to the rig.) Instead of an engine he had fitted her with a 19-foot yuloh, a long pole of Chinese origin that could be extended from the stern and gave the ship 1.25 knots when there was no wind. It was not until September 1931 that they set off for a winter in the Mediterranean. They spent a year there, most of it anchored off the island of Ibiza. In his book about the experience O'Brien began lyrically: 'It is the business of Yachts to discover Islands'. Islands had charmed him on his ocean voyages: the mysterious Trinidad and fog-enshrouded Amsterdam Island had had to be passed; Faial and the Falkland Islands had been refuges. Foynes Island had become his Irish home. Now with Kitty in the recently domesticated *Saoirse* he would find Ibiza, an island that would enshrine much that he held dear.

Initially they planned to spend Christmas in Ibiza, but once they got to the Mediterranean they dawdled. They stayed in Gibraltar nearly two months, then sailed slowly around the Spanish coast stopping at Cartagena. They spent Christmas in Alicante where it rained and they had to eat their tinned ham, sea stock sauce and Christmas pudding on the ship.

In *Voyage and Discovery* Conor claimed to feel uncertain about Kitty's allegiance to their spartan brand of yachting. He recorded their conversation as a vast Christmas cruiser passed them.

> I did not expect the mate's artistic eye to approve the decorations of the *Arandora Star*, but she might envy the comfort.
> 'How's that for a better kind of yachting?' I asked.
> She grabbed at the poop-rail to avoid being slung overboard by a frightful lurch as the wash of the tripper ship struck us and answered decisively – '*Saoirse* for me any day!'

They were disappointed with the number of northern Europeans in Alicante – it had a substantial fishing fleet but there was too much of a holiday atmosphere – and they entered Ibiza Harbour wondering what sort of a place they had pledged themselves to. They need not have worried. Ibiza

Conor on *Saoirse* in the Mediterranean. Pastel by Kitty Clausen c. 1932. Published in *Voyage and Discovery*, 1933.

in 1932 was still an unspoilt island dotted with working windmills, and the town, which clung to the hill on the southeast, seemed not to have changed for centuries.

O'Brien did not object to progress as long as it assisted rather than displaced traditional practices. Ice should be used for storing local fish, not to encourage a fishmonger to stock his shop with fish from Grimsby. Oxyacetylene welding was a godsend in a place where there was no coal, but assembling parts made in Detroit could not be counted as progress. It was a perceptive distinction, made at a time when nostalgia for the old in any form had taken a firm grip on the travelling middle classes. O'Brien valued the surviving crafts in their social

Pastel by Kitty Clausen for *Voyage and Discovery*, 1933.

tree that has grown the requisite number of tines … with the needful symmetry. I have mentioned the wooden or earthen buckets for the water-wheels. The shop doors are hung with baskets, mats, hats, ropes, and shoes woven, plaited, or spun from straws and reeds and the fibres of aloes and esparto. If all Europe foundered in a financial wreck this trade would not be in the least affected.[15]

Ever since his first encounter with the city of Pernambuco O'Brien had realised that it was the discovery of the old and still useful that he enjoyed and valued. He had no time for museums. 'I would give the whole of this [museum] for the door of the cathedral. The great brass handles of that are polished, not by the man who looks after show-cases, but by the many hands who want to go inside.'

Ibiza, with its narrow lanes, simple, asymmetric Gothic churches and haphazard flat-roofed houses appealed to his architectural taste. On his second visit to Pernambuco he had been struck by the way this Brazilian city outshone northern European and colonial cities: the Brazilians built 'not rows of houses but streets, not bunches of tenements but towns'. Because of the basic order there was room for exuberant rococo detail. He found similar qualities in Ibiza. St Dominic's Church 'has reduced church building to its elements, and left the field clear for church decoration. It is certainly as wide as it is high, and over the whole of the great smooth curve of the roof is painted a heavenly vision with hundreds of little figures in it.' The town itself was unplanned and his great delight was in the serendipitous discovery it provoked. 'We never thought when, approaching by sea, we feared there was nothing to be seen behind the pink-washed barracks that hid even the cathedral, that we should be embarrassed by the many beauties and interests packed within [the walls] … And we do not yet know all of them; every ascent of the hill is a voyage of discovery.'

context. He liked the way people still made things in their shops – plaiting ropes, knitting, embroidering, weaving baskets – while further back you could see where they ate their meals. He appreciated that shopping was regarded as an opportunity for social interaction. It was good etiquette to talk, and you maximised this by only shopping for one meal at a time. Most of all he admired the self-sufficiency so eloquently expressed in the ingenious ways the inhabitants compensated for the absence of iron:

> Observe the delightful shops that sell farmers' requirements … with the fastenings of harness cunningly contrived from crooks of wood, with hay-forks whittled out of a

A significant part of the revelation of Ibiza was that it was made with Kitty who revelled in the light and began to paint the landscapes in bold colour and simplified forms. She depicted the citadel by moonlight (Conor thought moonlight was unnecessarily theatrical for a place where sunlight reflected from the streets onto the walls gave it sufficient unreality) and exhibited it at the Royal Academy that summer. 'Citadel by Moonlight' became one of her best-known paintings. In it, *The Sunday Times* critic wrote, the 'pale buildings of the fortress are bathed in that blonde moonlight the subtle beauty of which has inspired many painters, but so frequently escaped attempts to capture.'[16] Conor was also inspired by the citadel and the defence of the town and wrote a short story about local privateers.[17]

Conor had great empathy for Kitty's painting. Seeing the boats tied alongside theirs on their first morning in Ibiza Harbour he anticipated her enjoyment: 'There is going to be plenty of fun for the artist among these schooners; she will enjoy painting them as much as they evidently enjoyed painting themselves. They like their colours bright and cheerful; no blacks and only enough grey to set off the deep white belt of their high bulwarks.' When he described the mountains behind Alicante it was in the first person plural with an artist's eye: 'We miss the suavity that grass and glaciers have impressed on our own landscape. Certainly these mountains are magnificent even at mid-day, but then they appeal to the orographer more than to the artist. They are not paintable till the half-lights of evening have simplified their modelling.'[18]

The apotheosis of their shared response to the Mediterranean was *Voyage and Discovery*. An account of their year on *Saoirse* written by Conor and illustrated by Kitty with a mixture of full-page pastels and inter-textual pen and ink drawings, it sprang from experiences shared, discussed and assimilated together. Sometimes the illustrations match a tone in the text that is not quite explicit. The ink drawing 'Embraced in the Market' extracts the humour of the situation in which Kitty met two acquaintances who embraced her simultaneously by depicting the moment just before the embrace when Kitty has dropped her artist's paraphernalia and the two friends, elongated, loom over her. Images and text might complement each other. Where Conor wrote about the colours of the harbour boats Kitty's black and white pastel emphasises

Pastel of Ibiza town by Kitty Clausen for *Voyage and Discovery*, 1933.

the overlapping and intersecting lines of the spars and rigging, giving the scene a modernist edge. Kitty displayed empathy for Conor's seamanship, depicting him taking in a sail in a high wind, the waves tall triangles, the sails distorted triangles and Conor a study of straining arms and legs.

The symbiosis of text and illustration make *Voyage and Discovery* a book of some considerable charm and give it an unmistakable air of happiness. This is underlined in Conor's closing lines: 'And we have to give *Saoirse* all the care we can; because, in case anything should happen to Iviza [sic], she must always be ready to carry us on another and a longer voyage. But I do not think she could make a happier discovery.' Underneath there is of course a light sketch of the ship, the sails furled, the crew lazily at ease.

Although Ibiza was not overrun by those escaping northern winters, it was not undiscovered by foreigners. There were artists, a few people wishing to make money from tourism or property, and tourists – the O'Briens immediately noted three foreign yachts in the harbour (French, English and Catalan) on their arrival – and the O'Briens soon got to know them. It was part of the loosely configured bohemian community that was establishing itself in southern Europe between the wars. Unlike their Victorian predecessors, these people stayed in the summer, revelling in the newly discovered physical delights of sunbathing and swimming. The O'Briens already knew at least one inhabitant of the Balearic Islands: Robert Graves, who had climbed with Conor twenty years previously, had moved to Mallorca in the late 1920s with the poet Laura Riding.

Conor and Kitty were drawn towards a German soldier-turned-sculptor, who lived by 'chicken farming, fishing and the capture of dragons' and also acted as a pilot. When they returned in 1934 they met a female German painter who, in partnership with an Italian, had set up a pension. The Italian married an American woman during the O'Briens' stay and asked them to act as a witness in the ceremony. 'We hardly even knew them by sight when they asked us. We are much flattered', Kitty told her parents.[19] She and Conor had 'the reputation of being the most solid & respectable people in the place.' Despite their artistic pursuits and informal clothing, Kitty and Conor did not quite slip into the bohemian category. Maybe Conor's insistence that they maintain the routine of meals whatever the weather while they were sailing was continued in port and gave them a staid image. There is a story that they dressed for dinner every evening. Or their reputation may have derived from their quiet compatibility, the solidity of their relationship.

After they left Ibiza they went to Barcelona where Conor's sister Kitty and his 23-year-old niece, Brigid (Dermod's daughter) joined them. Brigid, a painter, was given the status of cabin boy, but was keen to be useful on deck. Together they cruised the coast, visiting Algiers. They returned home in the autumn.

Voyage and Discovery was published in 1933. Kitty continued to exhibit, though her paintings did not sell as well as she hoped they would.[20] Conor had published his first technical book on sailing, *The Small Ocean-Going Yacht*, in 1931,[21] following it with *On Going to Sea in Yachts* two years later. They spent time in Falmouth, Cornwall: Kitty painted 'Harbour of Falmouth by Moonlight'. They were back in the Mediterranean in 1934. This time they left Ibiza for the Greek islands where Kitty painted ecstatically.[22] The following February they were in Vigo. A year later Kitty was dead; she was 50.

We have no record of Conor's reaction to her sudden death. It coincided with the outbreak of the Spanish Civil War and the ending of their Mediterranean idyll. In *Voyage and Discovery* Conor, aware of rumours of war in Spain, had written categorically, 'The old City will see no more fighting.' Ironically, Kitty's obituary on 10 August 1936 in *The Times* shared a page with a report of the recapturing of Ibiza by the Spanish government on 8 August just less than a month after the outbreak of fighting.

The Beaux Arts Gallery in London organised a memorial exhibition for Katharine Clausen in November 1936. 'Citadel by Moonlight' was there along with a melancholy oil of Snowdonia, the exuberant 'Fig-tree in Spring' ('standing out like a giant candelabrum against the colour-pattern of the landscape') and her flower paintings and portraits.[23] It was her landscapes that won through for, bold and vigorous, they had a transcendent quality. She had taken her father's sensitivity to light and colour and made it her own.

TWO BOYS GO SAILING

CONOR O'BRIEN

THE RUNAWAYS

By

CONOR O'BRIEN

Illustrated by

T. H. ROBINSON

The great C...
almost leger...
South Ant...
Andesia. T...
Basil and ...
into fact, an...
that followe...
giant fish.

Gold prospe...
battles aga...
forces of N...
woven in th...
tamed forest...
of South Ar...

A seven-foot streak of copper and gold flashed
in the sunlight

THE LUCK OF THE GOLDEN SALMON

CONOR OBRIEN

Illustrated by Robert Johnston

THOMAS NELSON AND SONS LTD
LONDON EDINBURGH PARIS MELBOURNE
TORONTO AND NEW YORK

Chapter 12
Author

Conor would make no more voyages in *Saoirse*. There was the expense, and in the late 1930s the world was becoming an increasingly difficult place in which to sail. Instead he wrote.

From Kitty Clausen's death until his own sixteen years later, he produced a steady stream of books: at least four more on the technical aspects of small-boat, deep-water sailing and at least five adventure stories. They were, with one exception, published in England. Oxford University Press took on the technical books. Slim, the text well set out on good quality paper, and with simple typographical covers, they are notably attractive books. Illustrated with Conor's finely drawn and clearly labelled technical drawings they are authoritative, but, written in the first person in a disarmingly informal style in which he advises from experience rather than lays down the law, they would have had a broad appeal within the yachting community and there were reprints.

By the early 1950s, O'Brien was an unashamed champion of old boats. In the preface to the reissue of *The Small Ocean-Going Yacht* of October 1949, Conor wrote, 'In the 19 years since this book first appeared many ocean voyages have been accomplished successfully, and many more have been abandoned at the first port of call. But I find little reason to revise my views, for the most successful vessels were those of the oldest type.' Whereas in the early 1930s O'Brien advocated a relatively uncharted type of sailing, by the early 1950s his was a lucid voice arguing for designs and methods that were being challenged by the advent of new materials (notably

fibreglass), industrial production and a return – with increasing prosperity – to large professional crews. *Deep-Water Yacht Rig*, published in 1948, was a classic, and remained popular even when the technology it described was superseded.[1] His credentials as a yachtsman with formidable ocean-going experience were kept before his audience by the reissue of the accounts of his voyages: the second edition of *Across Three Oceans* was reprinted in 1947 and *From Three Yachts* came out again in 1950. This experience was vital for his appeal, as was the fact that his design solutions were relatively simple and cheap.[2]

O'Brien found a formula for fiction in the mid-1930s, and his first adventure story, *Two Boys Go Sailing*, was published by Dent in 1936. He wrote two more stories soon after which were published in the early years of the war, *Atlantic Adventure* and *The Runaways*. After the war he published a further two: *The Castaways* and *The Luck of the Golden Salmon*.[3] All these books were illustrated with line drawings. His niece, Brigid Ganly, who was making a name for herself as a painter – she had painted the building of the Ardnacrusha power station in County Clare in 1927 – illustrated *Two Boys* and *The Castaways*; the established illustrator T. H. Robinson, who painted early twentieth-century inventors, illustrated *The Runaways*; and the artist Ellis Silas, who specialised in marine pictures and had caused a sensation in 1934 when his canvas of the First Dutch War was hung at the Royal Academy, illustrated *Atlantic Adventure*.[4]

O'Brien probably benefited from the success of Arthur Ransome's sailing stories for children – *Swallows and Amazons* was first published in 1930 – although he was writing for young teenagers rather than children. His books, without psychological insight, are plot driven. They

Three editions of Conor O'Brien's books for teenagers.

Cover illustration of Conor O'Brien's book, *Two Boys Go Sailing*, illustrated by Brigid Ganly and published in 1936.

invariably feature fifteen-year-old boys who are resourceful, independent, adventurous, self-absorbed, and skilled as sailors and climbers. Parents and guardians are well meaning but remote and allow the boys their freedom. The boys encounter indulgent grown-ups who respect and encourage the boys' adventurous spirit, sometimes against their better judgment. 'They had taken on a big job and ought to be properly equipped for it', reasons the navy commander in *The Runaways*, who suspects the boys have stolen their ship. There are references to the contemporary world: Irish republicans on the run, communists, exploitative entrepreneurs, the British Navy. But there is an aura of innocence, derived from the boys' self-absorbed enthusiasm for adventure and their desire to help adults they regard as vulnerable; they rub up against the world but are not apparently affected by it.

Aspects of O'Brien's experiences easily translated into boys' adventures. The books were set in South America and Ireland, had public school-educated heroes, revolved around the highs and lows of sailing and climbing, included rebels on

the run, storms, and local legends. He used the books, mostly unobtrusively, as another vehicle for preaching his gospel of small-boat sailing and for promoting his ideal of the simple self-sufficient life. Of Basil in *The Luck of the Golden Salmon* who had stayed in 'Andesia' (an imaginary state in South America) instead of returning to school, O'Brien wrote: 'and, if he missed some of the advantages of a public school at home, he made up for it by learning languages as they are spoken and the art of living on his own resources in a primitive country.' The books only seriously grate with modern sensibilities when class hierarchies are asserted: Thady, the working-class Irish republican on the run who is a far better sailor than either of the boys in *The Runaways*, is addressed by the boys as Thady, but has to call them sir, and when one of the boys speaks of the other to Thady he refers to him as Mr Cochrane.

O'Brien enjoyed writing these stories and claimed not to have a specific audience in mind. 'I like the book', he wrote to George Clausen in December 1943 of a novel (*Atlantic Adventure*) he had just written, 'because (as you may guess) I wrote it to please myself, not for the market, and I think it was rather bold of Harrap's to print it at all.' However, they fitted a particular niche very well and he had sufficient following to enable him to keep publishing until his death. After that tastes changed and books for older children and teenagers either engaged with the real world or evoked highly imaginative fantasy worlds.

Although O'Brien's technical books had a very different readership from his stories it is easy to hear the same writer in both. If one of his fictional teenage heroes had written on sailing he would have adopted the same practical tone as O'Brien. Writing both types of book O'Brien was escaping to the sailing and climbing he loved; clothing these activities in adventure and practical competence in the books he could appreciate in retrospect what he had lived so intensely in the 1920s and early 1930s.

Adventure was not entirely over for O'Brien. When the Second World War broke out in 1939 he joined the Small Vessels Pool, a voluntary civilian service of small-boat owners, who manoeuvred

Selection of Conor O'Brien's sailing books.

boats up and down the British coast and escorted small ships across the Atlantic. Given the rank of sub lieutenant, he worked with some remarkable men who had extensive, and in some cases very similar sailing experience to himself and who, like him, were now excluded from the regular navy because of age or illness. A photograph in the *New York Times* on 20 July 1943 showed O'Brien in the company of five men who were about to sail an American fleet tender to England.[5] The recently retired admiral Sir Herbert Meade-Fetherstonhaugh from Northern Ireland had had a distinguished career in the First World War commanding the cruiser *Royalist* in the battle of Jutland, and destroyers in the battles of Heligoland and Dogger Bank, winning the Distinguished Service Order in 1915. Samuel Evitt had worked on a submarine for the Royal Naval

Volunteer Reserve in the First World War.[6] The older men in the group had experience of making a living after retirement: two of them ran farms. They all wore white navy uniforms, whereas O'Brien, who was not sailing with them, had a darker uniform, shirt and tie, but with the epaulettes of a lieutenant. O'Brien sits in the front row, upright, with a moustache and, at 63, easily the equal to the naval men.

His wartime activities finished soon after this. 'It wasn't my fault that our show broke down & I was sent home after a very pleasant holiday with pay – such pay it looked, too, till I came to pay my bills, and I left the country no richer than when I arrived there', he wrote to George Clausen in December. He had visited the circumnavigator William A. Robinson, who was living on his unfinished ship,

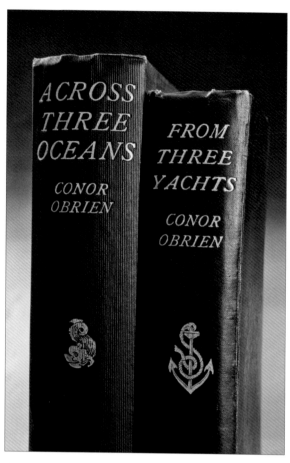

Conor O'Brien's most popular sailing books.

would have died out by the time it came to rebuild London after the war, another prediction which did not come true.

In December 1943 Conor returned to St Anthony-in-Roseland in Portscatho, Cornwall, reluctant to accept the slowing down imposed by age:

> So now I'm on the beach again, doing odd jobs at home, without any wage or inducement to travel as far as Newbury [where George Clausen now lived]. I have actually made an assignation in Tahiti with a man I met in U.S.A., and I have a chance of going there in a big sailing yacht, but I feel it in my bones that I shall never start. It is so much easier to write about the adventures of my story-book people than to undertake my own. A terrible confession of being too old at 63! Perhaps I only make it because the weather is so beastly cold. I shall feel braver in the summer, & change my mind about that voyage: anyway it can't come off till this war is over, and my yacht-owner, and his yacht, may have disappeared by then.[8]

He had sold *Saoirse*, but had not lost contact with the yacht. The new owner was a chartered accountant from Surrey, Vincent Ruck, whom O'Brien had met in America.[9] O'Brien sent Ruck a closely written letter on 4 January 1941 replete with *Saoirse's* details: sizes, repairs, materials, mechanisms.

> The chart room has 5'9" headroom –
> The bunk shown is narrow, but I always sleep there when at sea. There is a good deal of storage space under the floor for space blocks; also 2 big lockers under the cockpit, not too dry, because the cockpit though self-draining is not watertight.

It was a farewell to *Saoirse* in which all her features and all the time spent with her were lovingly recalled. It was also a generous gesture, initiating the new owner into the intricacies of his new possession. Conor ended pragmatically, asking Ruck to meet him on board so that he could take away domestic fittings 'which may be of value but which you don't want.'[10]

Varne, at Ipswich, Connecticut (dubbed by O'Brien 'vacation-land'). He spent some time in New York, 'the most fantastically beautiful city ever built.'[7] New York at that time was dominated by steeples, cupolas and towers, many in brick and terracotta: the Woolworth Building, the Municipal Building, the Empire State, One Wall Street. Individuality, which O'Brien had always admired in architecture, ruled: 'the oldest of them are the best. I thought the Woolworth building the finest tower I have ever seen. Alas! There are some "modern" ones of what I should call studied ugliness, so huge that they eclipse the others and destroy the fantasy of the skyline with horrid square blocks.' He confidently assured George Clausen that this 'cubist craze'

The Church of Ireland church in Foynes where Conor O'Brien's funeral service was held.

Why did he sell *Saoirse*? Once the war had started and he was away with the Small Vessels Pool, *Saoirse* needed to be berthed and looked after, expenses he could probably not sustain. The sadness in his letter of December 1943 when, back in Cornwall, his war work over, he found himself without *Saoirse*, suggests that perhaps he regretted selling her.

O'Brien spent his last years on Foynes Island. On the mainland the village of Foynes, with its deep harbour, had always had the potential to leap suddenly into the modern world. It had done this unexpectedly just before the war when it had been used for the newly developed seaplanes (also known, in reverse, as flying boats) in preference to nearby Rineanna, later Shannon Airport. Oil was stored in bulk near the quays, and direction-

finding equipment was set up on Foynes Island. The terminus was particularly busy during the war, but after 1945 airplanes took over at Shannon and Foynes' brief celebrity was over. However, the port continued to flourish. Foynes had become an awkward hybrid: an essentially rural village visited by vast container ships and framed by a multiplicity of cranes. In an odd way it matched O'Brien with his international reputation living his simple, often self-neglecting life within the protective presence of his sister Margaret and her family. When he was not writing he built boats. He continued to go barefoot and preferred to be without a shirt.[11] Lunch was often a lump of cheese and a bottle of Guinness, and in the evening he rowed across the sound to drink in Foynes. He collected his pension at the post office in the village. He was reserved, but pleasant, and

Loghill Church, County Limerick, where Conor O'Brien is buried.

Conor O'Brien's coffin arriving in Foynes after a short trip by boat from Barneen, Foynes Island, 1952.

he had plenty of companions. He was regarded as eccentric, and stories still survive of Conor of the Island who swam to Foynes with his clothes on his head.[12] He sometimes worked with Michael and John Finucane, and John rowed Conor's boat in the annual regatta.

Conor was healthy until the last months of his life when he developed heart disease. During this time John Finucane came to sleep in Barneen to keep him company. Conor died on 18 April 1952 of a coronary thrombosis. His body was placed in a coffin and rowed over to the mainland where four men carried it up the wooded hill to the single-celled, rubble-stone Church of Ireland church, built in 1926 when large numbers of Protestants were leaving Ireland. For many mourners it was their first time in a Protestant church, and Michael Finucane, who had carried the coffin, felt trapped when he found that the service had started before he could leave. O'Brien was buried with his parents a little further down the estuary in the cliff-top graveyard at Loghill Church, his grave marked by a limestone plaque simply carved by Seamus Murphy. Today the surviving battlemented church tower and the attendant graves are almost hidden in the wood perched directly above the waters of the River Shannon.

Abbreviations

NLI   National Library of Ireland
TCD   Trinity College Dublin
NAI   The National Archives of Ireland
NA   The National Archives London
JKMM Jim Kemmy Municipal Museum, Limerick
SMCA St Mary's Cathedral Archive

FTY   *From Three Yachts*
ATO   *Across Three Oceans*
VAD   *Voyage and Discovery*

CO'B   Conor O'Brien
DO'B   Dermod O'Brien
EC   Erskine Childers
EO'B   Edward O'Brien
JO'B   Julia O'Brien
KC   Kitty Clausen
NO'B   Nellie O'Brien

References

Introduction

1 Both O Brien and O'Brien were used in Conor's published works. The name given on his 1939 passport is 'Mr Edward Conor Marshall O'Brien (Conor OBrien)' and he signed it 'Conor OBrien'. I have used O'Brien throughout.

2 20 June 1923, NLI.

3 'Yesterday's News In Pictures', *The Irish Times*, 21 June 1923

4 There is now more scholarly attention being paid to Charlotte Grace O'Brien and Dermod O'Brien, see Anne O'Connell (bibliography).

5 There is one short biography by Pádraig de Bhaldraithe in Irish, see bibliography.

Chapter 1

1 See Davis and O'Connell.

2 Essay by Charlotte Grace O'Brien quoted in Gwynn, pp. 28–9.

3 Gwynn, p. 37.

4 William Smith O'Brien left the estate in trust to his wife to prevent it from being confiscated if he was convicted of treason.

5 O'Mahony, p. 3.

6 Jeanne Sheehy describes Cahirmoyle as a predominantly Romanesque Venetian style. See O'Brien Papers: Edward William O'Brien, TCD for building specifications and costs. The house was built between 1871–4 by John Ryan & Sons, builders.
See O'Keefe for information about the stone used in the house.

7 Julia bequeathed 24 Roland Gardens, London SW7 and Shalford, Guildford to Edward O'Brien who left them to Dermod, will, 22 October 1908, TCD. James Garth Marshall of Headingley House Yorkshire and Monk Coniston, Lancashire, in *Burkes*.

8 Birth Certificate.

9 12 March 1881, NLI.

10 2 December 1881, NLI.

11 7 December 1881, NCI.

12 'To Facilitate the Purchase of their Holdings by Tenants in Ireland'.

13 Gwynn, p. 37.

14 *Ibid*. p. 43.

15 EO'B to JO'B, 20 March 1881, NLI.

16 *FTY*, p. 196.

17 The family album was put together by Conor's sister Margaret and is now in the possession of her son, Murrogh O'Brien.

18 Mannix Joyce, 'Charlotte Grace O'Brien', *The Capuchin Annual*, 1974, p. 328.

19 *Ibid*. The graveyard is on Knockpatrick and is visible for miles around.

20 O'Brien papers, NLI.

21 23 January 1902, NLI.

22 Information from Suzanne Foster, archivist, Winchester College.

23 This is not conclusive, for university societies did not always keep records.

24 Saddlemyer and Smythe, p. 352.

25 JO'B to EO'B, 29 December 1900, and 1902, NLI.

26 JO'B to EO'B in O'Brien papers, NLI.

27 *Two Boys Go Sailing*, p. 99.

28 Robinson, p. 39.

29 9 August 1888, NLI.

30 Robinson, p. 44.

31 JO'B to EO'B, 26 June 1902, NLI.

32 *VAD*, pp. 125–6.

Chapter 2

1 In December 1901 Conor, contemplating a visit to Ireland, admitted that it was some time since he had been there. Family holidays to Cahirmoyle had probably ceased some years previously.

2   Dated drawings in *The Architectural and Topographical Journal Record* articles.

3   Much restored. Rev James O'Dowd, *History of St Mary's Cathedral, Limerick*, Limerick, revised edition, 1936.

4   Vestry Minutes, SMCA.

5   CO'B to DO'B, 21 January 1907, NLI.

6   30 March 1907, TCD. There was some discussion about the iconography of the central panel: 'It is strange indeed that they should stick at having St Patrick when the Church of Ireland makes such a point of claiming him,' Nelly wrote to Dermod. The Dean won that argument for when he presented the mosaic design to the Select Vestry in November 1910 it was of three figures of Christ as prophet, priest and king. (SMCA.)

7   Carved by M. Pearse & Sons, Dublin.

8   Vestry Minutes 10 November 1910, SMCA.

9   *The Architectural and Topographical Record*, three editions of the 1908 journals.

10 This was recognised by *The Building News*, 5 June 1908, p. 806.

11 Conor O'Brien's Senate bid, 1925.

12 CO'B to DO'B 15 March 1909, NLI. He worked here until at least 1914. CO'B became a member of the Royal Institute of Architects of Ireland. Green Book, 1912–1913, p. 29, Irish Architectural Archive.

13 Letter from CO'B 7 November 1912, creamery archives, NAI.

14 CO'B to builder, 15 July 1912, NAI.

15 Will, 22 October 1908, TCD.

16 *Cork Examiner,* 4 August 1961.

17 Boylan, p. 37.

18 Dickinson, p. 58. Conor also wrote a satirical verse on the episode reproduced in Dickinson pp. 88–9.

19 N[elly] to D[ermod] 7 June 1907, TCD.

20 O'Curry College of Irish provided Irish courses in the summer months and domestic economy courses for girls in the winter. See Paul Murphy, *Cuchulain's Leap: A History of the Parish of Carrigaholt and Cross*, Ennis, 1992.

21 *The Evening Sun*, New York, Friday 4 June 1915. Nelly toured with it to Iowa, Springfield Illinois, Sioux City, Chicago and New York. She organised events, publicised them, dined with governors and, dressed in an approximation of old Irish dress, gave public lectures and spoke to the press. She was fund raising for Carrigaholt and looking for support for the Gaelic League, already well known in some cities, in new places.

22 Nelly to Lucy Hyde 19 January 1915, and Nelly to Douglas Hyde, 17 March 1915, both in de Valera Public Library, Ennis, Co Clare.

23 Referred to in *Irish Naturalist's Journal*, 1946. Information from Pádraig de Bhaldraithe.

24 *Irish Builder,* 2 March 1912, p. 125.

25 The mountaineer and BBC producer Graham Hoyland, who instigated the expedition that found Mallory's body in 1999, presented a paper to the Royal Geographical Society on Wednesday 3 October 2007 arguing that Mallory and Irvine did reach the top. He believes that Noel Odell last saw Mallory not at the Second Step, as is usually assumed, but at the Third Step, a place from which they were more likely to have reached the summit. Ed Douglas, 'Did Mallory make it? Researcher believes he has the answer,' The *Guardian*, 29 September 2007.

26 Information from Suzanne Foster, archivist, Winchester College.

27 Robertson, pp. 86–7.

28 See Geoffrey Winthrop Young, 'An Impression of Pen-y-pass, 1901–1920,' in Carr and Lister.

29 Robertson, p. 86.

30 Robert Graves, *Goodbye To All That*, London, Jonathan Cape, 1929, Penguin, 1960, p. 57.

31 Carr and Lister, p. 79.

32 'Home Exploration,' *Climbers' Club Journal*, New Series, Vol 1.2 [1913], p. 47.

33 'Irish Mountaineering', *Climber's Club Journal* New Series, Vol 1.1 [1912], p. 90.

34 O'Brien, [1913], p. 50.

35 *Ibid.*, p. 48.

36 Brendan O'Brien, 'Winthrop, Young and Mallory on Brandon,' 11 August 1992.

Chapter 3

1   *FTY*, p. 57.

2   Details of the rowing boat in *On Going to Sea in Yachts*, p. 9.

3   CO'B to DO'B, 9 December 1901, NLI.

4   *FTY*, pp. 36–42.

5   Lloyd's Register.

Chapter 4

1   CO'B to EC, 31 July 1914, TCD.

2   *The Framework of Home Rule.*

3   Bulmer Hobson was a chairman of the Dublin Centre of the IRB and had played a major role in establishing the Volunteers, which he and his fellow IRB men hoped to dominate. They were frustrated in this at exactly the time of the gunrunning when John Redmond successfully asserted his authority by adding 25 Irish Parliamentary Party nominees to the provisional committee. Hobson accepted this to avoid a split, but in the process alienated more uncompromising IRB men. Not only was O'Brien baffled by unexplained identities but there were layers of complication of which he and the London committee were unaware.

4   List of Subscribers in Martin, p. 35.

5   Lyons, p. 325.

6   CO'B, 'Contraband of War,' in Martin, p. 111.

7   22 May 1914, in Martin, p. 37.

8   3 August 1914, TCD.

9   Hobson in Martin p. 138 says that John Dolan was the name to which Childers could write letters at an address in College Street, Dublin.

10 Martin, pp. 128–138.

11 See letters to Childers in TCD and his accounts in Martin and *FTY*.

12 'Contraband of War', *Irish Red Cross Junior Annual*, Dublin 1947 in Martin p. 111.

13 Martin p. 117–18.

14 Molly Childers to Alice Stopford Green, Martin, p. 99.

15 Diarmid Coffey in Martin p. 188 describes George Cahill and Tom Fitzsimons as 'paid hands', which was highly unlikely, and Kitty O'Brien 'as good as a man'. Mainchín Seoighe in *Portrait of Limerick* (London, Robert Hale, 1982 p.75) quotes a local song that names the men who had become local heroes.

> The Kelpie was the good yacht's name that
> sailed from Foynes one day,
> On a secret mission eastward bound to the
> silent Cold North Sea
> 'Twas summertime and Conor O'Brien, who
> owned and steered her too,
> With Tim Fitzsimons from the Island, and
> George Cahill as his crew.

16 *FTY*, p. 7.

17 Martin p. 118.

18 Mary Spring Rice, 'Diary of the *Asgard* 1–26 July 1914,' in Martin, pp. 68–97. Letter, Molly Childers to Alice Stopford Green, Martin, pp. 98–100.

19 29 July [1914], TCD.

20 For the two accounts see Darrell Figgis, 'Rendezvous at the Roetigen Lightship,' Martin p. 112 and O'Brien, 'Contraband of War,' Martin, p. 65.

21 There was some debate about whether O'Brien took too few arms. Childers and his crew claimed that they expected him to take half, but O'Brien publicly maintained that he took the proportion they had decided on. Martin, pp. 79, 101, *FTY*, p. 14. O'Brien told Childers that Figgis had prevented him taking more cartridge boxes. 31 July 1914, TCD.

22 3 August 1914, TCD.

23 CO'B to EC, 2 August 1914, TCD.

24 *FTY*, p. 21.

25 CO'B to EC, 3 August 1914, TCD.

26 *FTY*, pp. 22–3. CO'B to EC, 2 August 1914, TCD.

27 F. X. Martin (ed) *The Irish Volunteers 1913–1915*, Dublin, James Duffy & Co Ltd, 1963, p. 43.

28 p. 117. O'Brien kept one of the guns as a memento, letter to EC, 3 August 1914, TCD.

Chapter 5

1   See Thompson and Kerr and Granville for different opinions.

2   CO'B to DO'B, 14 February 1910, NLI.

3   RNR records, ADM 240/39, NA.

4   Thompson p. 95. Log of *Lord de Ramsey* August 1916 – 2 November 1916, NA.

5   RNR records, *op cit.* and information from Captain Roger Heptinstall RN.

6   Log of *Twilight*, 13 December 1915 – 17 August 1916, NA.

7   4 April 1917, RNVR Record, NA

8   Log of HMS *Kildare* 11 September 1918 – 9 December 1918, NA.

9   Thompson, p. 333

10 Martin, p. 110.

11 Proposed 10 September 1919, elected 20 September 1919. Information from Christopher Thornhill of the RCC Archive. The Cruising Club of 1880 became the Royal Cruising Club in 1902.

Chapter 6

1   Mrs Costelloe was the owner of 76 Waterloo Road, Thoms Directory, 1915.

2   The 1911 Census reveals that Robert Vere O'Brien (the father of Hugh Vere O'Brien) owned three of the six houses on the island. The others were owned by James Fitzsimons, Mary Sheehan and Michael Duggan.

3   Information from Michael Finucane.

4   *The Irish Builder and Engineer*, 24 October 1914. The hall still stands, heavily restored, and is the only building that can be attributed to O'Brien. The memorial commission probably came through his uncle Donough, an active member of the Vestry.

5   Conor had been given a draft but found the description of Dean O'Brien's contribution to the fabric of the cathedral imprecise and misleading from an architectural point of view. He suggested changes, some of which were made. CO'B to DO'B, 6 January 1915, NLI. The simpler wording of his suggested text for the dedication was not used. Several times during his leave from the navy during the war O'Brien was presented with cathedral problems.

6   Information from Suzanne O'Brien. Robinson, p.183. JO'B to EO'B, 30 January 1902, NLI. Inscription, St Mary's Cathedral.

7   The lettering is similar to the inscription *Saoirse* on O'Brien's yacht, though with slightly more pronounced serifs. Three plaques were added later under Aubrey's inscription; to Cicily Maud O'Brien, wife of Donough and their daughter, to Donough O'Brien and to Lucius' wife Emily.

8   Proposed in March 1920. Drawing, JKMM. The drawing includes Dickinson's name though he had gone to England after the war. Formerly the congregation, situated in the transepts, had been visually separated from the choir and clergy whose stalls filled much of the nave west of the transepts. Orpen and O'Brien's plan moved the clergy and choir in front of the transepts and brought the congregation into the body of the church. A limestone screen was to be erected behind the stalls separating them from the chancel, and the pulpit was brought forward closer to the congregation. It created a well-defined area for the service, more suitable for a smaller congregation. This reorganisation was financed by a gift from Viscount Glentworth and his sister Lady Victoria Brady. Vestry Minutes, 23 March 1920, SMCA. The limestone screen, and the bronze grille and gates, the latter not completed until May 1930, are the only lasting elements of this work. These are now situated one bay further to the east than they were placed originally.

9   Hilary Pyle (ed), *Cesca's Diary 1913–1916*, Dublin, The Woodfield Press, p. 230.

10   Senate bid, 1925, newspaper. See record in NUI Galway.

11   Mitchell, pp. 90–92 for a description of the fisheries during the First Dáil.

12   *FTY*, pp. 43–4.

13   Mitchell, p. 91.

14   Dáil Éireann, *Minutes of Proceedings, 1919–1921*, Government of Ireland, 1994

15   *FTY*, p. 45.

16   CO'B to DO'B 9 December 1920, and *FTY*, p. 73.

17   27 March 1921, NLI.

18   Robinson, p.131.

19   29 May 1919, NLI.

20   12 April 1921, NLI. Report in *Limerick Chronicle* 9 and 12 April 1921.

21   *FTY*, p. 89. *Kelpie* had gone onto a reef. She had stayed there on one tide but was broken by the next. *FTY*, p. 64.

22   CO'B to DO'B, 29 October 1922, NLI.

23   There is no chapter by Conor in *The Voice of Ireland*, published in 1924.

Chapter 7

1   Maurice Griffiths, *Swatchways & Little Ships*, London, Adlard Coles Nautical, p. 107.

2   Conor Cruise O'Brien, p. 38.

3   *FTY*, p. 93.

4   *VAD*, p. 122.

5   *Saoirse* is described in *ATO*, *FTY* and *The Small Ocean-going Yacht* and in Hiscock.

6   *FTY*, pp. 99–100.

7   *Saoirse* was registered 6 June 1922 at Limerick Custom House. Building started on *Saoirse* in October 1921.

8   *FTY*, p. 126.

Chapter 8

1   For example, flying records were set in 1927 when Colonel Charles A. Lindbergh Jr. flew solo across the Atlantic.

2   *FTY*, p. 144.

3   Recorded in the log. The extant logbook (private collection) is a transcribed version of the log he would have kept on the voyage. A cloth-covered book, about 10 inches high and 12 inches wide, it has a printer's reorder label glued onto the endpaper dated 20 October 1923, three months after O'Brien set out on the voyage. The entire log, written mostly in pencil, is in Conor's hand, which is consistent and neat. It covers the round-the-world journey, the *Ilen's* voyage to Port Stanley, the 1927 Fastnet race and journeys in the Mediterranean with Kitty Clausen. Most of the entries concern the mechanics of sailing – wind direction and strength, barometric pressure, course, direction and average speed – set out in columns. There is very little on the life lived by the inhabitants of the boat. Conor probably transcribed the log as a prelude to writing his accounts of the voyages.

4   Logbook.

5   Mitchell, p. 87. If Smith-Gordon was still managing director of the Land Bank in 1923 this may mean that the Free State contributed financially to O'Brien's voyage.

6   A legal contract between the seamen and captain.

7   The ship was registered in Ireland but as the Irish Mercantile Marine was not yet recognised *Saoirse* came under the provisions of the British Merchant Shipping Act.

8   *ATO*, p. 24.

9   *ATO*, p. 32.

10   *ATO*, p. 18.

11   *ATO* (2nd edition, 1931), p. 28.

12   *FTY*, p. 143.

13   CO'B to DO'B, 27 May 1924. NLI. *ATO*, p. 21.

14   CO'B to DO'B, 3 December 1923, NLI.

15   Sidney Lavelle, 'The Cruise of the *Saoirse*: Pernambuco to the Cape – From Day to Day', *The Irish Times*, Saturday 3 November 1923.

16   Conor O'Brien, '*Saoirse*: "Boa Viagem!"', *The Irish Times*, 1 November, 1923.

17   Shakespeare, *Macbeth*, Act 1 Scene iv: reference to Thane of Cawdor: 'nothing in his life Became him like the leaving it'.

18   *The Irish Times*, 2 November 1923.

19   3 December 1923, NLI.

20   *Ibid.*

21   *ATO*, p. 97.

22   *ATO*, p. 117. In the logbook he records that they had taken 'sundry trunks and bags'.

23   *The Argus*, Tuesday 19 February 1924, p. 11. I am grateful to Pádraig de Bhaldraithe for lending me extracts from the Australian press.

24   CO'B to DO'B, 27 May 1924, NLI.

25   *ATO*, p. 124–5.

26   *ATO*, p. 125. He also signed on R Flaherty, logbook.

27   CO'B to DO'B 27 May 1924, NLI.

28   18 May 1924, NLI.

29   27 May 1924, NLI.

30   22 June 1924, NLI.

31   CO'B to Margaret O'Brien, 8 August 1924, NLI.

32   *FTY*, pp. 144–5.

33   Letter dated 28 March from the Acting British Consul at Pernambuco to the Board of Trade about Captain O'Brien's report. Letter dated 6 April 1925 from 'Yacht "Saoirse" at Pernambuco' to the Hydrographer of the Navy. Correspondence from Pádraig de Bhaldraithe who received it from the Hydrographic Data Centre, Hydrographic Office, Ministry of Defence, Taunton, Somerset.

34   The discoloured water is marked on chart 2202B.

35   Griffiths, p. 107.

36   *The Irish Times*, Monday 22 June 1925. Racing had been suspended for the day.

37   *ATO*, p. 263. Conor presented a chart to the United Arts Club, which was later stolen.

Chapter 9

1   CO'B to DO'B 11 January 1926, NLI.

2   There was a second edition in 1931, an impression in 1947 and a third edition in 1949. It was reprinted in 1968 by Hart-Davis and again by Granada in 1984. It has been translated into French.

3   Preface, second edition *Across Three Oceans*, 1931, published in London by Philip Allan & Co Ltd, for their Nautilus Library. The most prolific author for this series was J. G. Lockhart whose books included *Mysteries of the Sea* and *Peril of the Sea*.

4   Conor O'Brien in *The Irish Times*, 18 October 1924.

5   *FTY*, p. 168.

6   *FTY*, pp. 176 and 201.

7   *ATO* (2nd edition), p. 17.

Chapter 10

1   Monare was the address of his correspondence from the island. He shared Barneen with another family.

2   Information from Murrogh O'Brien and Michael Finucane. The dinghy remains on the island.

3   Information from Murrogh O'Brien.

4   Terence Brown uses this phrase in *Ireland A Social and Cultural History 1922–1985*, London, Fontana, second edition, 1985, pp. 94–5.

5   Southern Unionists were guaranteed special representation.

6   There are now plans for a museum focused on *Asgard*. Alicia St Leger's *A History of the Royal Cork Yacht Club* was published by the Club in 2005. The return of *Ilen* in 1997 was followed with interest in the press.

7   Griffiths, p.108

8   *FTY*, p. 180.

9   Griffiths, p. 110

10 In April 1928 he told Dermod that one of the thrillers had failed to find a publisher but he had higher hopes for the second, 11 April 1928, NLI. One of these may have been 'The Philosopher's Stone,' manuscript in NLI.

Chapter 11

1   10 August 1936.

2   'Six Lectures on Painting,' 1904 and 'Aims and Ideals in Art,' 1906.

3   Prizes: silver medal, painting from life 1910, prize for design for a figure picture in 1911. Royal Academy archivist.

4   *Morning Post*, 24 November 1936.

5   2 April 1934, private collection.

6   George Clausen to DO'B, 22 September 1928, NLI. She also exhibited at The Glasgow Institute and The Society of Women Artists.

7   George Clausen to DO'B 30 April 1917, NLI is the first letter in the collection and is particularly polite. George Clausen exhibited at the Dublin Arts Club, the predecessor of the United Arts Club, in the late 1890s.

8   Reproduced for the frontispiece of *From Three Yachts* where it is dated 1927 and on page x of this book.

9   This was to take place after a brief trip to Spain with Francis Macnamara, a wild poet and philosopher, who was paying the expenses and initially intimidated O'Brien ('frightened of my first view of Macnamara but I think we shall get on all right') and Romilly John, Augustus John's son.

10 O'Brien Family Album.

11 *VAD*, p. 87.

12 *Ibid.*, p. 126.

13 *FTY*, p. 168.

14 Hugh Clausen to E.V. Ruck, 3 November 1967.

15 *VAD*, p. 146.

16 29 November 1936.

17 'The Corsairs of Iviza', Ms in NLI. Conor was inspired by a monument in the modern harbour that commemorated the taking of the English privateer barque *Felicity* in 1806 by Xebec Vives, the best-known but not the last action of the Iviza corsairs. Kitty painted the streets and gardens of Ibiza, the harbour at Andraitx in Mallorca. 'Late Sunshine, Iviza' was exhibited at the Royal Academy in 1932, and a year later one of her entries was 'The road: Iviza to Sta Eulalia.' A watercolour, 'Sunlight and Almond Blossom', a Mediterranean landscape with local life in the foreground – a horse and cart carrying sacks, two priests and a peasant woman – was reproduced in *The Studio*, copy in O'Brien archive in NLI.

18 *VAD*, p. 99. He described the 'pale warm grey stones' of the Straits of Gibraltar 'shining golden in the full sunshine, later glowing with orange fires till these were quenched by pure cobalt blue spreading out of the deep ravines.' *Ibid.*, p. 30.

19 Kitty Clausen to her father and mother, 2 April 1934, private collection.

20 George Clausen to DO'B, 13 February 1936, NLI.

21 Reprinted 1951.

22 'The Isle of Santorini', 'Gulf of Sparta'. Kitty Clausen to parents, *op. cit.*, George Clausen to DO'B, 13 February 1936, NLI.

23 *The Times*, 23 November 1936.

Chapter 12

1   Griffiths, p. 110.

2   Even today O'Brien's advice about rigs and cleats is quoted on the web for these reasons.

3   By December 1943 he had another manuscript that he could not get published because of the paper shortage: *The Castaways* was eventually published in Dublin by Browne & Nolan in 1946.

4   Brigid Ganly, RHA, 1909–2002. There was a
    retrospective of her work at the Hugh Lane Gallery
    in 1998. She painted landscapes in Ireland and
    Tasmania, flowers and still lives. T. H. Robinson
    (1869–150), Ellis Silas (1883–1972). Silas's 'The Price
    of Glory' depicted the First Dutch War.

5   A tender serviced a larger boat.

6   There were two army men, Colonel Gunn and
    Lieutenant Colonel Newland, who had been in the
    Royal Artillery. Newland had fought in the Boer
    War. They were aged between 63 and 66 whilst Sir
    Richard White who had been invalided out of the
    army, was only 33.

7   CO'B to George Clausen, 17 December 1943, private
    collection.

8   *Ibid.*

9   Hugh Clausen to E. V. Ruck, 31 December, 1967,
    private collection. *Saoirse* was sailed by Vincent's
    son Eric, who later became the owner.

10 He was writing from St Mawes (near St Anthony-in-
    Roseland) where he planned to beach *Saoirse* when
    conditions allowed him to get the necessary repairs
    done. Ruck gave him £250 for the boat, which
    Conor shipped to St Just.

11 Information from Michael Finucane.

12 Information from John Cussen and Arthur Quinlan.

Select Bibliography

For unpublished sources see Notes

Published works by Conor O'Brien

Across Three Oceans: A Colonial Voyage in the Yacht Saoirse, London, Edward Arnold & Co, 1927

Atlantic Adventure, London, G. G. Harrap & Co, 1943, with illustrations by Ellis Silas

'Barony of Bunratty Upper, Parish of Quin', *The Architectural and Topographical Record*, vol. 1, part 2 (June 1908), pp. 169–192

'Barony of Connello Lower, Parish of Askeaton', *The Architectural and Topographical Record*, vol. 1, part 4 (December 1908), pp. 249–308

'Barony of Islands, Parish of Dromcliff, County Clare', *The Architectural and Topographical Record*, vol. 1, part 2 (June 1908), pp. 141–168

Boats, Oars and Sails, London, Oxford University Press, 1941

Deep-Water Yacht Rig, London, Oxford University Press, 1948

From Three Yachts: A Cruiser's Outlook, London, Edward Arnold & Co, 1928

'Home Exploration', *Climbers' Club Journal*, new series vol. 1, 2 [1913], pp. 47–50.

'Irish Mountaineering', *Climbers' Club Journal*, new series vol. 1.1 [1912] (with Page Dickinson), pp. 90–96.

On Going to Sea in Yachts, London, Oxford University Press, 1933

The Castaways, Dublin, Browne and Nolan Ltd, 1946, illustrated by Brigid Ganly

The Luck of the Golden Salmon, London, Thomas Nelson and Sons Ltd, 1951, illustrated by Robert Johnston; 2nd edition 1952, reprinted 1956

The Practical Man's Cruiser: An Introduction to Deep-Sea Yachting, London, Oxford University Press, 1940

The Runaways, London, George G. Harrap & Co Ltd, 1941, illustrated by T. H. Robinson

The Small Ocean-Going Yacht, London, Oxford University Press, 1931, 2nd edition 1949

Two Boys Go Sailing, London, J. M. Dent & Sons Ltd, 1936, illustrated by Brigid Ganly

Voyage and Discovery, Edinburgh and London, William Blackwood & Sons Ltd, 1933

Yacht Gear and Gadgets, London, Oxford University Press, 1945

Secondary Sources

Boylan, Patricia, *All Cultivated People: A History of the United Arts Club, Dublin*, Gerrards Cross, Colin Smythe, 1988

Burke's Irish Family Records, London, Burke's Peerage Limited, 1976

Carr, Herbert, C. and Lister, George, A. (eds), *The Mountains of Snowdonia in History, the Sciences, Literature and Sport*, London, Crosby Lockwood & Sons Ltd, second edition, 1948

Chichester, Francis, *Along the Clipper Way*, London, Hodder and Stoughton, 1966

Childers, Erskine, *The Riddle of the Sands: A Record of Secret Service*, London, Smith, Elder & Co, 1903, London, Penguin Books, 1978

Davis, Richard and Marianne (eds), *The Rebel in his Family: Selected Papers of William Smith O'Brien*, Cork, Cork University Press, 1998

Dear, I. C. B., and Kemp, Peter (eds), *The Oxford Companion to Ships and the Sea*, 2nd edition, Oxford, Oxford University Press, 2005

de Bhaldraithe, Pádraig, *Loingseoir na Saoirse – Scéal Conor O'Brien*, Dublin, Coiscéim, 1996

de Courcy Ireland, John, *Ireland's Sea Fisheries: A History*, Dublin, The Glendale Press, 1981

Dickinson, Page, L., 'A Rock Climb in County Wicklow', *Climbers' Club Journal*, old series vol II, (1911), pp. 8–13.

——, *The Dublin of Yesterday*, London, Methuen & Co Ltd, 1929

Ferriter, Diarmaid, *The Transformation of Ireland 1900–2000*, London, Profile Books, 2004

Fitzgerald, Seamus, *Mackerel and the Making of Baltimore, Co Cork, 1879–1913*, Dublin, Irish Academic Press, 1999

Griffiths, Maurice, *Swatchways & Little Ships,* London, Adlard Coles Nautical, 1999, originally published by Allen & Unwin, 1971

Gwynn, Stephen, *Charlotte Grace O'Brien: Selections from her Writings and Correspondence with a Memoir,* Dublin, Maunsel and Co., 1909

Hankinson, Alan, *Geoffrey Winthrop Young: Poet, Educator, Mountaineer,* London, Hodder & Stoughton, 1995

Hiscock, Eric, *Voyaging Under Sail,* London, Oxford University Press, 1959

Holm, Donald, *The Circumnavigators: Small Boat Voyagers of Modern Times,* London, Angus and Robertson, 1975

Holzel, Tom, & Salkeld, Audrey, *The Mystery of Mallory and Irvine,* London, Jonathan Cape, 1986

Irving, R. L. G., *A History of British Mountaineering,* London, B. T. Batsford Ltd, 1955

Larmour, Paul, *The Arts and Crafts Movement in Ireland,* Belfast, Friar's Bush Press, 1992

Kerr, Lennox, J., and Granville, Wilfred, *The Royal Naval Volunteer Reserve: A Record of Achievement,* London, George Harrap & Co Ltd, 1957

Lyons, F. S. L., *Ireland Since the Famine,* London, Weidenfeld and Nicolson, 1971, Fontana, 1985

Martin, F. X. (ed), *The Howth Gun-Running and the Kilcoole Gun-Running 1914,* Dublin, Browne and Nolan Ltd, 1964

Mitchell, Arthur, *Revolutionary Government in Ireland, Dáil Éireann, 1919–22,* Dublin, Gill & Macmillan, 1995

Nixon, W. M., *To Sail the Crested Seas: The Story of Irish Cruising and the First Fifty Years of the Irish Cruising Club,* Dublin, The Irish Cruising Club, 1979

O'Brien, Conor, Cruise, *Memoir: My Life and Themes,* Dublin, Poolbeg, 1998

O'Connell, Anne, 'The Life and Work of Charlotte Grace O'Brien, 1845–1909', MA dissertation, University of Limerick, 1993

O'Keefe, James, 'History of Cahermoyle', *Journal of the Newcastle West Historical Society,* no 2, (1996), pp. 53–5

O'Mahony, Christopher and Thompson, Valerie, *Poverty to Promise: the Monteagle Emigrants 1838–58,* Darlinghurst, Crossing Press, 1994

Piper, Leonard, *Dangerous Waters: The Life and Death of Erskine Childers,* London and New York, Hambledon and London, 2005

Ring, Jim, *Erskine Childers,* London, John Murray, 1996

Robertson, David, *George Mallory,* London, Faber and Faber, 1969

Robinson, Lennox, *Palette and Plough,* Dublin, Browne and Nolan Ltd, 1948

Saddlemyer, Ann, and Smythe, Colin (eds), *Lady Gregory, Fifty Years After,* Gerrards Cross, Colin Smythe, 1987

Sheehy, Jeanne, *J. J. McCarthy and the Gothic Revival in Ireland,* Belfast, Ulster Architectural Heritage Society, 1977

Thompson, Julian, *The Imperial War Museum Book of The War at Sea 1914–1918,* London, 2005, 2nd edition, Pan, 2006

Index

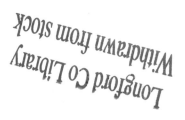